T0146524

IT'S ALL ABOUT
LOVE

Metaphysics Demystified
A Handbook for Life

FRAN WELLGOOD

BALBOA.
PRESS

A DIVISION OF HAY HOUSE

Balboa Press books may be ordered through booksellers or by contacting:

Balboa Press
A Division of Hay House
1663 Liberty Drive
Bloomington, IN 47403
www.balboapress.com
1 (877) 407-4847

Print information available on the last page.

ISBN: 978-1-9822-2588-9 (sc)
ISBN: 978-1-9822-2589-6 (e)

Balboa Press rev. date: 04/24/2019

Contents

Acknowledgments

I thank Life! Without this road that has been my life, I never would have walked through the fires that burnished me, but didn't kill me . . . surprisingly. I remember when I was told that life was a grand adventure, and I scoffed. Now I understand. It just takes life to understand. Along the way, my husband Edward, and my dearest friend Pamela loved me until I learned to love myself. They really taught me what Love is. I would not be who I am without them.

As difficult as my family life was as a child and adult, it was the first fire I walked through . . . and lived to tell the tale. I am grateful for that challenge. It set me up with the yearning to learn and know what is true and good. And out of that, my sister Ann emerged as the best friend who has walked with me my entire life. We both rose above what our family told us about Life, and chose Love.

My editor, Beth Landi, is the one who helped me craft all of my writings into this book. And the one who prodded me onto my path in North Carolina by telling me I needed to teach her Reiki shortly after I moved here. She has been an invaluable friend, guide and steered me through what seemed an overwhelming process.

Karen Romanchek is my dear friend who lovingly takes care of my body with her skillful massages. And it was during a visit with her that the light opened up and I heard my guides say, *It's Time! Time to get the book done!* She has the biggest heart!

My spirit, body and mind are also lovingly taken care of by Lisa Fields, my friend and amazing EMDR therapist who has guided me through putting together the pieces of my journey; Julia Wilkins, my Atlas Chiropractor par excellence and Esthetician Diane Mack who help me manage all the energy flows within and without; best yoga teacher ever Stephanie Barnhill who reminds me to be grateful for the body that serves me on and off the mat; Niki Gerds showed me how to develop my physical strength through weight training so I could continue to do energy work in a strong body.

Many heartfelt thanks to Elizabeth Michalka and Chris Dollar: my first friends in North Carolina who have witnessed all the twists and turns in this circuitous journey to today...and stuck with me anyway; and to Deb Morek, my dear friend whose heart holds me and my family with love and care and is always there for me in any and every way.

I am grateful for my California connections; all of whom have seen an even longer evolution and loved me through it all: Cynthia Rubin, Sharon Teitelman, Stephen Thal and Susan Richter. They all taught me about friendship, and of course, about Love and compassion.

I cherish everyone's love and support more than they know.

All of my clients and students have been instrumental in my evolution. I have needed all of you so I could do the work I love. Thank you for receiving what I have offered. In return, I have learned so much! My heart is full and grateful for you all.

Every former teacher, California, the real estate bubble that helped us get to North Carolina, the energy of Wake Forest and the amazing people I have met here are all part of my journey. My guides always told me, just hang on until 50. Don't opt out of life yet. The year I turned 50, we moved from California to North Carolina. And then my life all started to make sense and come together. I am so thankful I was so taken care of and guided, even when I couldn't feel it.

So, I suppose ultimately, I am thanking the Universe/Life/Spirit/All That Is/Source/God/Love for all of it. It was all necessary to bring me to this moment . . . and to bring this book of writings to you. I offer it to you with all of my heart and all of my love.

Preface

It took me many years (decades really) to understand and resolve how Metaphysics is All About Love. The simplest definition of metaphysics is: beyond (meta) the physical (physics). For me, this means understanding that we are more than this body and this human life. It means that we are energy, first and eternally, and that energy is Love. And while I may have explored—even clung to—metaphysics at first out of desperation, the study and practice ultimately opened me to the possibility and then to the experience of a life of love and peace, right here on this earth, right now.

I was introduced to metaphysics at 16. Now I look at that event as the loving hand of Spirit, the Universe, All That Is, Source Energy . . . whatever God is to you . . . guiding me. By that age, I had told the Universe if this is what life is, I want out. I didn't understand that the purpose of life was to *know the Love that I already am and thus be in joy* because my life was devoid of joy. I was ready to bail this vale of tears. In hindsight, I could hear my angels and guides say to me: Really, Fran? This lifetime you could work through so much of your old baggage, you could resolve old issues you've been carrying around, learn how powerful you are, and learn to love yourself! Maybe you should stick it out. We'll direct you to people and tools that could help you. Not that you'll always hear us or even know we're guiding you and watching over you!

Ultimately, though, it was my choice. We all have free will. Fortunately, I was desperate enough and in enough pain to pursue something that seemed to hold Light and Truth—and ultimately, Love.

Along the way, I found some teachers, I read a lot and, indeed, I was guided and directed, although I often felt no one was listening and no one was there for me. I learned that I was part of a loving Universe even when I couldn't feel it. I learned that just getting through life in one piece was evidence that I was taken care of. And the more I used all that I had been taught and all that I read, the more I lived and applied these ways of thinking and being, the more I learned how to respond to life with grace. It wasn't about stopping the waves of life. It was about learning I could surf the waves better. That was living in grace and love, for myself first. Then I could extend that love to others.

My practices, first in California, included bodywork, energy work, and teaching metaphysics. My energy work and teaching of Reiki and metaphysics later in North Carolina grew and transformed as I grew and transformed in my understanding of and commitment to living a life of love—in a practical way. I already knew that these seemingly abstract, esoteric-sounding principles had a real life that could be applied in real life. And real life could include more joy, more ease, more compassion. Who knew?! So, as I wrestled with my issues and found I could help other people with their issues because I was in the trenches, too. The resolutions stemmed from love and it started with loving myself. I held on to that awareness over the years of struggle, and as I turned 50 and moved to North Carolina and began my practice, I came to understand even more clearly the wisdom and intelligence of the life that lives through us. I came to understand all of this was simple, but not easy. I learned to ask myself first, in every situation, what is the most loving thing I can do for myself here? What is for my highest good, and that of all concerned? These became my guiding principles.

Weaving "metaphysics" into my life became a daily practice, and it was a practice. Like anything else, it took time to incorporate it as a seamless part of my life. I didn't have to be there 100 percent—51 percent got the job done. As humans, we will never be 100 percent aligned 100 percent of the time with our energy. Our energy is our Higher Self, our Soul, our Spirit, the Loving Energy of which we are an individual part. We strive for 51 percent. And every time we are willing to use and be that love, through our words, our deeds, our intent, our affirmations, we lay in a gossamer wing of love. We often can't even feel them until they reach 51 percent, and suddenly, we are at the feeling of love, of trust, of knowing something is already taken care of, of knowing we are always taken care of, held in the palm of Love.

We are imperfect humans, as we are meant to be! This lifetime is about learning we are love, loving ourselves, circulating love and good feeling to ourselves and others, and allowing that love to be expressed in a myriad of ways through our talents, skills, abilities, and compassion, for the purpose of being in joy. As we do that, we let go, gradually and over and over again, of what might be in the way of allowing ourselves to feel that orbit of love. We become willing to have compassion for ourselves and others. We allow ourselves to be in this flow of love and realize this lifetime is a balance of being and doing. We have a lifetime to learn and practice this. It's not once and done.

We are guided along the way by the Universe, our angels and guides, our inner wisdom. These are all part and parcel of the Loving Energy that we are. We all might perceive this energy in different forms, and it doesn't matter how or if we see or feel any of this. It is the undercurrent of life. We are joined at the hip with all of the Universe. We are a drop in that ocean that is the Universe, a particle of sunlight of the sun. And it takes all of us to make up the ocean, the sun, the Universe. As we push or pull, the Universe moves with us. As we ask for help, knowing it's already there for us and receiving it in the same breath, the Universe responds lovingly, in a way that is for our highest good, not necessarily how we think it should respond! We begin to let go of anything we might be holding on to that is in our way of receiving what is for our highest good. We begin to be more present, which allows us to be more connected to our Higher Self, which is the Love we are. And as we practice that more, as we let go more, as we surrender to our Higher Self more and more, we hear our guidance, our inner wisdom more clearly. And then we begin to see that life is much more supported than we think. There's more guidance and assistance than we thought possible.

All of this is much simpler than our human minds make it and, at the same time, it's not easy.

We can move into love all through the day, for seconds or minutes. We keep asking, what is the most loving thing I can do in this situation? Maybe you have a meditation practice; maybe you talk to whomever or whatever in Spirit as you drive to work every day. We can ask for help with everything. Spirit is equal opportunity and doesn't judge anything as less or more important. Whatever you are going through is your path, and your own way to learning about love, and one of the ways we stay present is by staying on our path and off other people's paths. We mind our own business. And when we focus on our path, we then begin the practice of forgiving ourselves.

As we are willing to expand our awareness of ourselves as more than the body, as part of Spirit, as loving beings that will return to the Loving Energy from which we came, we find life falls more into perspective. We are aware that our path is for our benefit, we can only know about our path and no other, and that we come here to circulate love and good feeling, to ourselves first. This is not selfish; it is essential self-care. We fill up with that loving feeling and spill it over to everyone and everything around us.

These are some of the life lessons I talk about in this book. My intention is that you could open this book anywhere and whatever you are moved to read at that moment is what might benefit you in that moment. There are actual mechanics to aligning yourself with the loving flow of energy that we are, which helps us to live this life in an easier, smoother way. I've attempted to communicate these as I have practiced, resolved and understood them. I offer them for you to integrate into your understanding and application for you and your life.

Through my study of Chinese Medicine, I came to see how we are aligned with the energy of the seasons, and how we can use that to support us through the year. The energy pouring into the earth plane has increased over the last few years, urging us to be aware of our loving, energetic selves and encouraging us to make choices to align more and more with that love, often by presenting difficult worldly circumstances. Yes, life can seem overwhelming and there are always infinite possibilities. As we open to our spiritual nature, we become more aware of our true capacity, and can feel less overwhelmed by our human difficulties. And find the grace to respond to them.

As far back as I can remember, my mantra was that I wanted a meaningful life. I didn't have a clue what that meant, except I wanted to heal and teach. What I discovered was that when we realize and feel the Love that we are, then all of it, everything we do and all that we are, is meaningful. It's all in the service of learning that we are love, we learn how to love, and we are loved. It all circles around, over and over, ever expanding into more love. Right in the middle of this crazy world of ours. We learn that life flows through us. And it's not about what's happening around us; it's about our response to it. And first, we need to teach ourselves to love ourselves, which is the path to healing. I found that I needed to teach myself to remember Love in order to heal. In that light, "We are the ones we've been waiting for," an idea attributed to a Hopi elder, makes all the sense in the world.

I was told many years ago that no matter what I was told or taught, I would have to resolve it for myself, make it my understanding. I found this to be true. I couldn't speak with authority or credibility about anything that I hadn't worked through and resolved and understood for myself. I rely on your inner wisdom and discernment to consider what I have written and use what is for your highest good. You will know in your heart of hearts. You will know what is loving for you.

I love this blessing from John O'Donohue's book *To Bless the Space Between Us*. I have shared this many times, and now is the next perfect time. It is one of my favorites and touches my heart every time I read it. Let it fall into your heart. This is what it means to be All About Love:

To Come Home to Yourself
May all that is unforgiven in you
Be released.

May your fears yield
Their deepest tranquilities.

May all that is unlived in you
Blossom into a future
Graced with love.

Your Guiding Word

Toward the end of every year, I start thinking about my guiding word for the year to come. This is a word or phrase to help guide me, keep me focused and on track, and inspire me throughout the year. My guiding words have included Joy, Embrace, Limitless, Infinite, Peace and Self. Our word presents itself when we ask our true being, our Higher Self, our inner wisdom. We all have our answers within us.

To open up to your guiding word, simply and curiously inquire: what is the word that is a guiding light for me in this new year, this new cycle? Just let it rise up without judgment. Just ask, take your time. You may be surprised at what comes to you. It may take a few days or even into the new year, but at just the right time, you will hear it.

But what if you can't hear it? Don't worry. It doesn't mean that you don't have a guiding word or that you don't have an inner voice. It may just mean that you have to grease your channel a little bit. The channel to your inner being may be a bit rusty from lack of regular conscious use.

Try sitting quietly. Imagine the light that is your true being, with all your answers, sliding into the top of your head and settling inside you, getting very comfy merging with your physical counterpart and radiating beyond your body. Now, as much as you can, just let go into your light and imagine the year ahead. Ask what guidance your inner voice/inner being has for you without efforting. You might even playfully ask, is this it? with words that come up that you think you might like.

Start opening the channel by having the conversation with expectancy, but not effort. Allow your mind to wander over the upcoming new year and without attachment or agenda, just ask, and receive. Trust yourself. A friend whose mind is always active questioned whether the word she heard was being given to her by her true inner voice or her active thinking mind. When I suggested trying other perfectly good words, they just didn't fit like the word that managed to be heard through all the daily mind chatter. Trust that you really do have access to your true inner voice. It always manages to be heard some way, somehow.

The word you receive will unfold during the year. It will take you to many different places and have many permutations that may not be obvious at first. But it will absolutely guide you. The year that peace was my guiding word, I thought that I would be guided to find peace in any situation. Instead, I came to realize that I was already peace, but I wasn't always willing to be what I already naturally was. And that was a great part of my guidance and learning that year.

Wishing you joy and ease in the process and adventure of unfolding your guiding word.

Teaching of Joy and Resistance via Skype

Blessings come in such strange disguises. My guiding word a few years ago was Joy. My word came up as I was talking with someone about their word. After their word popped up, I was saying how I hadn't really spent any time yet asking for mine and then, there it was. When someone hears/feels/senses their word for the year, I usually ask them to try on one or two other words that might seem like perfectly good choices. Once THE word has surfaced, though, nothing else quite fits. Other words just don't have the resonance of the word that has presented itself as your word; they don't have the same "legs" or stability. You can feel the difference. And I could tell that joy was clearly my word.

Now, you might think I'd be joyful at having the word joy, but surprisingly (even to me) I was a little miffed. Joy? Me? I AM joyful. Surely, I didn't need any guidance in that area. I talk about it all the time. Then I began to get it. Talking about it is not owning it, not feeling it. And as we open to deeper and deeper layers of all that we experience and understand in life, and the learning is as infinite as the Universe, as is Spirit, I could certainly open to deeper experiences of joy, infinitely deeper experiences of joy, and I could certainly use a daily reminder. It's so easy to fall off the "joy wagon" and start believing all the human joylessness that is presented to us daily.

So naturally, I was presented with opportunities to release resistance to the infinite flood of joy available to me, to allow more joy into my experience daily. One of these little golden opportunities was using Skype. My sister had sent me a webcam because she wanted to Skype with me and I had not gotten around to the simple set-up procedure. I didn't have time. I didn't want to make myself presentable for the webcam. I don't like being on camera. I like the invisibility of the phone. My sister was patient. And finally, as I simply entertained the thought and feeling of joy and my willingness to embrace more joy, I developed the desire, effortlessly, organically, naturally, to hook up the camera and try Skyping.

My nephew in Oklahoma was my first test. I called him just as he was going home (of course, this was unfolding ever so smoothly) and very shortly, I was seeing him and his kitty on my computer screen, and getting used to seeing me on camera in a corner of my screen. That was a little disconcerting, but soon we were being so silly and laughing so much I could hardly talk! We had much more fun talking via Skype than I might have had on the phone. It was a much more joyful experience. Imagine that! And yes, I Skyped with my sister later and had a wonderful time.

Wondrous, miraculous occurrences happen every day because we are a part of the Divine energy that creates infinite possibilities. Simply by entertaining the idea of joy and not worrying about the details of it, I had a perfect opportunity to choose joy and release resistance, and thus experienced more joy than I could imagine—in the form of Skyping. Who knew?

That's the point. We don't have to know. Just focus on what we want, not what we don't want. And that desire is always answered, sometimes in very surprising ways.

Here's wishing you more joy than you can imagine!

Touching the Divine

Whether we're aware of it or not, we are always connected with the Divine, Source, Spirit, God, Oneness. But periodically we break through all that's in our way and feel who we really are. We feel that inextricable connection with our true nature. Sometimes to a greater or lesser degree, but it's unmistakable.

The most unlikely thing could be a trigger for the opening—a piece of music, the quietness of morning when the rest of the house is still asleep, the purring of a cat, the trust and awareness that all is unfolding perfectly, no matter what it looks like. Sometimes I feel the wave of loving indivisibility just sitting at the computer appreciating this visible expression of energy flying through the ether.

When I feel this liquid wave of love, my heart fills with love for everyone and everything. Unconditional love is loving the perfect, whole and complete spirit of everyone, not the fallible human. And no matter what our faulty human is doing, everyone's Higher Self, everyone's true being, is pure loving light.

Our work in this lifetime is to learn to align with the loving beings that we naturally are. And when we remember our Divine nature, we can go on and more gracefully navigate this vale of tears. May we all come to know ourselves as radiance.

Eye of the Needle

If it's spring and you're feeling a little pushed, squeezed, or bent out of shape, you're right on track. The upward moving, forceful energy of the season is guiding you, or maybe manhandling you, depending on what you're experiencing.

The foundation for this pure, high-vibrating energy was laid in 2012 and 2013. Now it's time to welcome and integrate this energy that pushes us to be our most authentic selves. This means being willing to hear or be made aware of what is for our highest good, what will assist us in living in our highest integrity. This also means that every bit of old baggage that we have been carrying around and that has been weighing us down is coming up for review, forgiveness and potential release.

Spring energy is very flexible. In Chinese Medicine, the element of spring is wood, the green, flexible, sapling wood of spring growth. Green wood bends in the wind, gives with the stresses and flexes, but doesn't break. So, although this might be a challenging time as we are pushed to and past our limit of intimacy with ourselves, we won't break. We are just being asked, by our own loving self, to examine our current life and thoughts and only keep what is part of our essential, loving, compassionate nature, and let everything that is unlike love fall by the wayside. Only that loving essence will fit through the "eye of the needle" which is this portal, this gateway, this spiritual crossroads into the new season.

Here Comes the Sun

The doyo, in Chinese Medicine, is the 10 days or so before and after the change of seasons, and a time of sometimes painful transition and transformation.

During the days leading up to the Summer Solstice, the day with the most hours of sunlight, we are moving from the wood element of spring to the fire element of summer. We are evolving from the thrusting energy of spring, of wanting to bring balance and order out of chaos, into the possibility of joy, intimacy and warmth of the summer season as we celebrate the beauty in everything. It is the time to rekindle our fiery passion for life.

As we are part of Spirit, which is infinite, our capacity to experience all qualities of loving life is also infinite. And just as we think we trust, there is more trust to be had and to plunge into head first. Or to paraphrase American spiritual teacher Ram Dass: It doesn't matter if we have a parachute or it doesn't open, there is no ground.

The illumination which is pouring into the earth plane and into our lives lights up all our nooks and crannies of resistance, and we are asking ourselves to release anything that is in our way to knowing and welcoming our own inherent radiance. No more excuses, no holds barred, with our infinite capacity.

Know you are not alone, no matter how severe your challenges feel. We are all in this together, threads of the grand and beautiful tapestry we call Life, Source, God, Spirit, the All. And it is and we are only Love.

Everything is Perfect

There's a lot of talk (including by me) of connecting with your power. What that really means is to connect with the Love that you are, and that connection gives you the power to love you, take care of you, and embrace your responsibility for you. All of us are always in some phase of learning and applying this.

I can tell when I'm connected with my true loving self, where I can so feel my alignment with All That Is, and the peace and gratitude that ensues, because then I truly know and feel that all is perfect no matter what it might look like from the outside. And I know that every moment before contributed to this moment, with all that it contains. And I embrace it all.

When we are mindful of the Light that we are, we are mindful of our true nature. In mindfulness, as we fill up with that loving feeling that nourishes our reservoir, we have a buffer to be more resilient to life's slings and arrows and waves. Not that the waves stop crashing in, we just learn to surf better.

California meditation teacher and author James Baraz says this about mindfulness:

"Mindfulness is the ability to be aware of what's happening within and what's happening all around you, in a state of acceptance. Acceptance does not mean agreement. Acceptance does not mean we sit idly by if action is appropriate. But by accepting the experience of the moment, we align with our inner compass and find the capacity to enjoy the pleasant and be with the unpleasant; to take clear action or rest in the present.

"Mindfulness is simply being aware of what is happening right now without wishing it were different; enjoying the pleasant without holding on when it changes (which it will); being with the unpleasant without fearing it will always be this way (which it won't)."

Everything is perfect when we have the compassion to accept ourselves and our current experience as it is—perfectly imperfect.

Thanksgiving and Forgiveness

In Chinese Medicine, fall is the time of the metal element. We use metal to create infrastructure and sometimes the old infrastructure has to be torn down to make way for the new. In the fall, we "gather in" what we have grown during the spring and summer and sort that which will serve and nourish us in the winter to come. We let go that which is not up to snuff, that which will not nourish us during hibernation and rest. There is often grief in letting go, but letting go is necessary to make room for more good. We must create the space to allow for the receiving.

In the spirit of this letting go—and letting come—time, I share a forgiving practice called "Ho'oponopono" as discussed by Hawaiian psychotherapist and psychologist Hew Len. Forgiveness has been defined as ceasing to cherish the displeasure of someone or something. We let go of the displeasure we are holding. More letting go, in service of letting more good come into the void created by the release. Dr. Len says:

"In the ancient Hawaiian culture, whenever a member of the community fell into any kind of misfortune, whether through illness, accident, or even willful crime, the entire population sat in a circle around the person, silently searching their own hearts for how they may have contributed, even in some seemingly minor way, to the person's suffering. Perhaps they held a judgment against this person or their family or maybe felt a secret envy or jealousy. Whatever the case, after they recognized their part and silently asked for the subject's forgiveness, they quietly left the circle. No words were shared. In the end, when all had made their own peace, the individual sitting in the middle was healed.

"As simple as this practice sounds, it works based on what we now call quantum principles—that we are all entangled or connected and therefore we cannot escape the effects of one person on the collective or of the collective on one person. It also works on the metaphysical level, that of the One Mind asleep in the dream of suffering (our human lives). All minds, then, are joined as One."

Dr. Len has distilled this tradition of forgiveness, handed down from his elders, to four phrases: I love you; I am sorry; Please forgive me; and Thank you. He suggests beginning Ho'oponopono by thinking of someone or some situation that evinces a loss of joy, however slight. Hold this subject in your mind and repeat the four phrases, directing them to this mental image. You don't have to "feel" the connection; the feeling comes after the choice to do this. Spirit is more than eager and willing to heal this relationship—even as little as one percent of willingness from you opens the door.

Dr. Len describes the practice this way:

"**I love you**: We are recognizing that at a deep level we are One. We are mirrors for each other. Judging or condemning you would just be doing the same to me. You, in my perception of you, are a projection of my state of mind. Loving and forgiving you is also doing the same for me. The divisions between us are only in our imaginations. Although bodies and actions appear separate, the Mind that is expressing through all of us is the same. All behavior is either an expression of or a call for Love. So, Love is the cause of everything, and the cure at the same time.

"**I am sorry**: Not for anything in particular that you or I have done—that would make the offense real—but for together having decided to experience separation, and for all the suffering of all of us as a result of this mutual decision. For that I am truly sorry. And I am sorry for my contribution in this way to your particular experience of suffering, confident that in our awakening and acceptance of forgiveness, we shall ultimately see all suffering washed away in an instant of healing and liberation.

"**Please forgive me**: Not for what it appears I have done, but for agreeing with you to create this dream of suffering and separation. Please see me as an undiluted, invulnerable, eternal, and forever joyful Spirit who through the majesty of your own creativity and freedom has created this opportunity to awaken and remember Love, and I trust you to love me and forgive me my illusion.

"**Thank you**: For giving us both an opportunity to heal our relationship, to heal in my mind any misperception of you as less than Divine, knowing this healing goes out to the One Mind and affects everyone and everything in Creation beyond what we can imagine. Thank you for joining with me as One Mind and healing together.

"With this level of understanding," Dr. Len says, "simply repeat the four phrases with your subject in mind until you feel a shift or inner lightness around the relationship. That is all. You will find that when you next see this person (or are in the situation), something has changed. What has changed is that the veils of darkness between you have lifted. You are now both seeing more of your real selves in each other. The past has melted away in the Light of Spirit that you invited into the relationship."

Dr. Len has now condensed this practice to simply: I love you; thank you.

Thanksgiving is a good time to say I love you; thank you.

Blowin' in the Wind

For many, late fall is the season of letting go of old baggage, the stuff we have been carrying around sometimes for our lifetime. I have an image of this like the piles of leaves we see everywhere during this time of year. At first, we love all our stuff. We love to think of it, look at it, examine it, wallow in it. Likewise, we might love to jump into a pile of leaves and play in it. But after time, the leaf piles become dank and moldering as they gather moisture and slime, much like the old baggage we hold on to long past the time when it served our highest good. Finally, the leaves are vacuumed up or the wind does the job and vigorously blows them away. The streets are cleared, leaving space and openness behind. The trees now have light pouring through their branches, unhindered by dead leaves whose purpose in shielding the earth from the strong summer sun is now complete.

Like the trees, we are being stripped to our energetic bare bones. The season's energy scours the bottom of the barrels of our beings, scraping away the sludge and gunk that has sunk and congealed. As it rises up to be emptied, it doesn't look pretty or feel good. But it leaves an expanse of spaciousness behind to be filled with the light of the present as we release the muck and sediment of the past.

We are approaching the day with the least hours of sunlight, the Winter Solstice. The days are shorter now, the light is waning. But the old residue is being dropped from the trees and from our lives. It's being cleared out of the streets and out of our experience. Space is made, an opening is created in preparation for the day after the Solstice when the amount of light increases. The light continues to build daily as it approaches the Summer Solstice, the day with the most hours of sunlight. This growing, illuminating light offers to shine in our being, in our lives, day by day, if we just say yes, giving us the opportunity to fill the awaiting space with light. But first, we must let go in order to make room for more light. We just have to be willing. We can trust the intelligence behind the process; it is our natural process, too. The Light always follows darkness.

Ghosts and Goblins

We're living in a time of accelerated energy and that energy is bringing up the ghosts and goblins of our old ways of being. These patterns or deep grooves are outdated ways of thinking and acting, or reacting, that no longer serve us, are no longer aligned with our highest integrity. But if your experience has been anything like mine, these old skeletons that have been rising up will not be ignored.

Autumn is a time of sorting and letting go, and making room to receive more good. Thus, I find myself in the continual process of noticing the old patterns as they rise up, being willing to be grateful they are showing themselves so clearly, and being willing to let go, over and over and over again. And I forgive myself every time I speak or act or think in a way that is not of my Higher Self, my true nature of love and peace.

It's a constant practice, as is anything that we want to become easy and smooth. Once we have the awareness that this is the path of life, and are willing to notice what rises up, then we have the power to make a choice. And therein lies freedom and joy.

It's not that old stuff won't rise up like wraiths or apparitions; we are always clearing out and letting go. But in the space that is made, we can always choose Love.

My Moment with the Divine in Walmart

I once had a moment of experiencing our intrinsic, inextricable connection with the Divine in Walmart. It was the Sunday before Christmas and I was just shopping for household stuff. But I received a gift of infinite magnitude.

I was thinking about an email I had received some days before from a friend who was dealing with some very hard blows. She said she didn't feel heard or seen by God. I knew all was truly well, that she and her family were completely taken care of, that everything was working out for the good no matter what it looked like in the moment. And in that moment, I felt my/our indivisibility with the Divine, with the All.

I knew that just by virtue of being part of the loving energy of the All, of Source (and we can only be part of the tapestry of energy that exists), the All has to respond to us. When we pull on our thread, the whole of the tapestry responds to our tugging. The All doesn't resist. Our human selves may resist, but not Divine energy.

There is a saying I've never been able to attribute to anyone, but read a long time ago: "True love needs a response." We are true love, in our very nature, our true, Divine nature. When we ask, demand, request, tug at the All, there is absolutely a response. It cannot be any other way. It's almost as if Source has no choice. Think of it any way you like . . . as beloved children of God or of the Universe, which is only Love. However you look at it, our benevolent Source only responds with love, without any question or judgment. The response may not look like what we expect (with our human minds), but it will be the exact response we need for our highest good. And only given out of pure Love.

We can slow down the process with our doubt and questioning. We can get in the way of receiving the gift that is always there for us. We can temporarily keep the love and support of the All at bay. But all we have to do is surrender our resistance and say: Yes, thank you. Over and over and over again. The support and love and response of the loving Universe is limitless and infinite, whether we feel it or believe it or know it—or not.

Rumi, a 13th century mystic and poet, said: "Silence is the language of God, all else is poor translation."

I find myself unable to accurately communicate the feeling of absolute connection, support, partnership, response I felt that day at Walmart. These words are a poor translation of those moments of grace.

A Little Help from Our Friends . . .
or Asking and Receiving

It's hard to tap into gratitude or peace when we feel tested at every juncture. Sometimes life's demands become so taxing, we can feel stretched beyond our capacity. But of course, we have infinite capacity (as our Higher Self, the true, eternal part of our self) and it turns out that even if we don't remember or feel that part of our self, we get through everything with more grace than we thought we could. And we do stretch, we do expand, we do find more strength, more trust, more love than we thought possible. As Spirit is limitless and infinite, so are we. We just don't always remember.

In the spirit of being stretched, I am continually being pushed into really learning what it means to take loving care of myself. I kept telling my guides, I AM taking care of myself. And I kept hearing, Yeah, tip of the iceberg! My guides have such a sense of humor!

So, I make a practice of asking for help, with practically everything. We need to be willing to do whatever is necessary to really take care of ourselves and surrender stubbornness and ego in thinking we should, could, do it all on our own. That stance may need to be part of surrendering what isn't working. All of this process, that of needing help, guidance, assistance, is a continual lesson in asking for and receiving help. Of course, that which I teach is what I need to learn most: receiving. Not just asking, but receiving.

It is an art and a practice to receive all the guidance, support, answers, and help available to us from Source with its infinite solutions and resources. We can complicate the issue. We don't get out of our own way. We sometimes tend to make things more difficult than they need to be, often because we don't know how to do it any differently. We don't have the skills, or the understanding that if we allow, ask for and receive the energy of the Universe to support us, whatever we're working with can be easier. One of my favorite mantras in the morning as I set up my day is: I wonder how easy today can be. I love today being easier than I can imagine!

There are powerful currents flowing underneath everything we see, pushing things to resolution, connection, unveiling. We are one with All That Is and there is always a response to our requests—maybe not the one we expected, but always a response. There has to be! We pull and the universe responds. Now is the time to be willing to be unknowing, but sending out desires, eagerly anticipating whatever is for our highest good, better than we can imagine!

In her poem "Allow," poet Danna Faulds expresses this mix of surrendering, allowing, and receiving:

Allow

There is no controlling life.
Try corralling a lightning bolt,
containing a tornado. Dam a
stream, and it will create a new
channel. Resist, and the tide
will sweep you off your feet.
Allow, and grace will carry
you to higher ground. The only
safety lies in letting it all in —
the wild with the weak; fear,
fantasies, failures and success.
When loss rips off the doors of
the heart, or sadness veils your
vision with despair, practice
becomes simply bearing the truth.
In the choice to let go of your
known way of being, the whole
world is revealed to your new eyes.

— Danna Faulds

Ask, Allow, and Receive! With a little help from All of the All, always our friend.

Surrender

Surrender is one of those words that can really push a button. What am I surrendering? To whom or what am I surrendering? Why would I surrender? Aren't I supposed to be strong and stand up for me?

We surrender to our Higher Self, that wisest, most loving part of ourselves, our highest integrity. We surrender the way our human mind thinks it has to be. We desire things to work out a certain way, then we let it go and make space to receive what is for our highest good. That is what is truly meant by surrendering, in the best sense of the word.

When we surrender to our Higher Self, which is a bit of the Divine, a bit of the essence of the Universe, of All of the All, we embrace all that we are, All That Is. We are an indivisible part of Source energy, of the Universe itself. And the loving universe cannot be separate from us. It's at our backs, ready to support, guide and assist us without question. All we have to do is let go, surrender, and receive. Simple, but not easy.

This is the adventure of life. We have a lifetime to learn how to live our lives. It is all unfolding perfectly every moment. And when we surrender, get our human minds out of the way and allow life to flow through us, we are truly present and loving the ride.

Aligning with Our Higher Self

We come to this earth plane to remember that we are part of Loving Spirit. We come here to learn how to love ourselves so we can then love the good in everyone and everything else. The purpose of life is to be in joy, knowing we are part of Love. Our true work in this lifetime is to circulate that love and good feeling, to ourselves first. When we fill up with love and good feeling, we feel the harmony and joy and ease that we are, inherently, naturally—our true nature, our first nature. And then that spills over to everyone and everything around us, effortlessly. So simple . . . not easy.

Yogi Bhajan said: "Life is a flow of love, only your participation is requested. Love is the ultimate state of human being where compassion prevails and kindness rules."

How do we align with the flow of Love that we are, with our Higher Self? We need simple tools, techniques. One of my favorite methods is saying as often as possible during the day: I am willing to be more loving to myself than I thought possible. What would be the most loving thing for me to do right now, in this moment?

Trust the process, participate with your willingness.

We are Divine, but we are also living the duality of being human. When we have compassion for our humanity, and are willing to align with our Higher Self, our true nature, our first nature, then we feel the flow of Love that is life and is us. When we are willing to be present and inhabit each moment, whether or not we know what that means or what it feels like, we are allowing for and welcoming alignment with our Higher Self, the Love that we are. Then we feel the joy that we are and the joy that is possible to feel, even in this human vale of tears.

Filling Up and Spilling Over

One of the beauties of being present is that it makes it easier to align with our Higher Self. Byron Katie and Eckhart Tolle talk about being radically present, embracing what is presented in the present. Our work is always evident; whatever shows up in the present is where our work is for this moment.

Anything we become good at, we practice, and we practice coming back. Buddhist teacher Cheri Huber says: "With each moment, no matter what is going on, the practice is to find the willingness, the courage, the faith, and the compassion simply to come back to the present, come back to this heart, come back to this person, and not to give up just because it's difficult." And indeed, it is difficult, and still we come back, with compassion for how daunting that practice can be.

I think of being present as a constant "coming back," because, of course, we wander off the present moment over and over again. When we are willing to be present, and willingness is the key here, we clear the channel, the connection, the awareness between our conscious human mind and the pure joy and harmony of our Higher Self, our true eternal nature. Then there is no impediment to the Love that we are flowing into our present experience, even if just for a moment or a glimmer. When we are being filled by the wellspring of Love that we naturally are, we fill up and then we spill over that Love to everyone and everything around us.

When we and those we love are bathed in the infinite wellspring of Love, we are more able to feel the wholeness of us all, rather than the damage. In truth, our true beings, our higher selves, are whole, perfect and complete. But it's hard to remember and access that as we go about our daily human lives. When we take a moment to just breathe, and breath connects us with Spirit and our Spirit, or Higher Self, we remember in a small part of our being, perhaps for just a moment, that all is well, we are well, we are whole, perfect and compete.

As the song says, don't get fooled again. But we will. And we will have compassion for ourselves and we will breathe and we will come back to the present, once again, and to the Love we are.

Floating

What happens when we fill up with the Love that we are? When our reservoir is bursting and overflowing? Why, we float! To wherever we need to go and to whatever is our next step. We don't even have to know what that is. We just have to be willing to release what we might be holding onto that is unlike love. We have to let go of whatever is weighing us down, even if we can't identify it, and make space. After all, if the vessel is already full, we can't receive all the love the Universe and our Higher Self have to offer. For what purpose do we receive this love? To what end? To take us where we need to go for our highest good.

We release. We are willing to receive. And then we remember what our true nature is. When we circulate that love and good feeling, to ourselves first, we don't have to worry about the details, the plan, the visualization. Certainly plan, intend, visualize, if it contributes to your good feeling. But really, all we have to do is be willing.

Willingness is the key. It opens the door to the support of the Universe. It's how we say Yes! And yes, we also have to be willing to be uncomfortable as we try something different like staying present, releasing and receiving what is for our highest good while at the same time not knowing exactly what that is. We can trust the process, even if it feels uncomfortable temporarily. This will pass, in the right time, and we will feel our buoyancy. We will remember we are light, and we will float.

Resistance . . . and Allowing

When we let go of resistance, we are more present. When we are more present, it's easier to allow the Love that we are to flow through us into our bodies, lives and experience. This is how we can experience health, wealth and happiness, no matter what things look like. This is how we can begin to feel less affected by outside people, conditions and things. Sometimes these things seem impossible to experience! How do we let go of resistance?

All resistance is resistance to loving ourselves in some way. Read that again. All resistance is resistance to loving ourselves in some way. If we are feeling tight, restricted, unhappy, things are not flowing smoothly in our lives, we are somehow resisting the harmony we naturally are. Life is designed this way so we can feel the restriction and take responsibility that we are reacting to circumstances in some way, then choose to respond differently. Choose to trust in the face of the unknown. Choose to surrender to the wisest part of ourselves. Be willing to find the peace in the midst of the chaos, not stop the chaos. How do we do this?

We focus on what we want, not what we don't want. We don't focus on the fear, the unknown, the waves that are battering us. We acknowledge them, and we breathe and are willing to lean into them, move through them, ride them, knowing we are taken care of even if we don't know how. We can focus on being grateful for something, anything. We can ask: What would make me feel good right now? What can I do to be loving and kind to me right now? What would make my heart sing right now?

When we are experiencing something we don't like, we can actually bless the experience and question what were we just thinking? How were we just thinking? What shows up in our life is the indication or projection of the patterns of thinking or beliefs that we are holding (more than 51%). In that awareness, we have to choose some other way of approaching the problem to solve it - new thinking, create a new pattern that serves us better and brings a different result. We have to try something different, step out of our box that we may have created, out of our well-worn groove. Step out of our rigidity and resistance and allow something else, something different. We can try trust and love. Sometimes we just have to be desperate enough to try something so drastically different.

Each time we are willing to trust the Love that we are, that is part of All That Is, that has all the solutions and all the support and all the answers for us, we lay in a gossamer wing of love and good feeling. We might not feel it or believe it at all. This is where mantras and affirmations come in. The words don't change things, but they move us toward a new feeling. When enough gossamer wings get laid in, when they reach critical mass, we can finally feel them. We finally reach the 51 percent tipping point in our good feeling and the relief comes, the resistance evaporates. We feel the Love we are.

Co-creation, or the Mechanics of Manifesting Metaphysically

There are no happier people on this planet than those who decide that they want something, define what they want, get hold of the feeling of it even before its manifestation and then joyously watch the unfolding as, piece by piece, it begins to unfold. That's the feeling of your hands in the clay.

— Abraham

These are the "mechanics" of manifesting metaphysically. We desire something (this or something better, whatever is for our highest good). We reason, think about it, sort it out. We "do our part," or all that needs to be done about it in our human, visible world: the researching; the reading; the looking for the job or the place to live or whatever we desire. Then we let it go to the Universe, to Source, to Spirit, to All That Is.

We literally say, I let this go to be completed with my co-creative force, however you perceive it. And we work toward the 51 percent feeling that it is already done, simply by being willing (the key) to know and feel it already completed in Spirit, already done perfectly. We believe it before we see it. We make space to receive the resolution, the solution, the answer. And when we are 51 percent sure (and we may not even be aware that we are there!) and willing to receive, the answer appears. It may not be what we expected, but we are always answered.

Saying Yes to Healing

Zen master Thich Nhat Hanh says we "inter-are." We are part of everything else. His "I Am That" exercise reminds us we are a part of everything, part of the Oneness. Everything, including us, makes the Oneness. We are indivisible from the All, but individualized in our human, visible expression.

We don't function all on our own. We can't do it all on our own. For those of us in the business of helping others heal, this is a particularly hard lesson to accept. We come smack up against our ego. Somehow, we want to think we don't need the help others need, that somehow, we should be able to do it all alone if we were really accomplished healers. So not true. That's just the ego speaking. But usually, we have to be brought to our knees to reach out and ask for and, even more importantly, receive and say yes to the help we, of course, need like everyone else. Putting ourselves on pedestals benefits no one, least of all ourselves. We all have feet of clay. After all, we are human as well as Divine.

Following a life-changing health diagnosis, I was willing to take loving care of myself, or so I thought. We do things in baby steps. I am no exception. So, since the diagnosis, I have inched my way toward expanding my idea of what it means to take loving care of myself, and accepting the healing modalities available to me. (A dear friend once told me I was the most stubborn person she knew. I was mystified. I had a lot to learn.)

My Higher Self and the Universe took things (and me) in hand later when I was felled once again. And finally, I surrendered. Finally, I let go. Finally, I said I have no idea what to do, how to heal, I give up and ask for and receive help. I said Yes. And the healing energy flowed in to guide me through the next steps. And it entailed reaching out and asking—and receiving—help.

I eventually garnered the most wonderful group of healers in a loving sphere around me. Among them were massage therapists, chiropractors, reflexologists, acupuncturists, intuitives, yoga teachers, and doctors, as well as all my students who teach me while I teach them. I realized what an amazing swirling energy vortex I have right here where I live with so many highly skilled and caring health and energy professionals.

I recall during one acupuncture treatment, the peace and connection that had been eluding me in the weeks prior flowed into my heart. I was so grateful I had dropped my resistance, that I had said Yes, that I had allowed myself to receive. Being willing was as much a part of my healing as the actual treatments and people, which were symbols in and of themselves of the loving answer Spirit was giving me in response to my request.

I am properly humbled by my need for assistance from others. I love the orchestration of how I and all these people came to this area and found each other, all guided by our inner wisdom. We just have to listen. Little did we know what connections would be revealed for the highest good of all concerned. The Universe must be delighted with its handiwork. I know I am. And I am eternally grateful.

Interrelationship

You are me, and I am you.

Isn't it obvious that we "inter-are"?

You cultivate the flower in yourself,

so that I will be beautiful.

I transform the garbage in myself,

so that you will not have to suffer.

I support you;

You support me.

I am in this world to offer you peace;

you are in this world to bring me joy.

— Thich Nhat Hanh

Suffering is Optional

When you think everything is someone else's fault, you will suffer a lot. When you realize that everything springs only from yourself, you will learn both peace and joy.

— Dalai Lama

Someone emailed me this quote and asked what it meant because it seemed to place "blame" on the individual. I thought this was a great question because there's a difference between blaming ourselves, which causes suffering, and taking responsibility, which empowers us.

Blame is a human way of thinking of things. Responsibility is what the Dalai Lama is talking about here, which is our divine choice. When we take our power back, own that everything we experience HAS to come from us (where else could it come from if we're experiencing it?), then we are powerful because then we can make a choice. We can then see that we are reacting to something, which is giving our power away.

Blaming someone gives your power, your joy, your good feeling away. When you realize you have the ability to respond, the response-ability (responsibility), rather than react, then you are powerful. . . then you choose not to suffer, because then you can make a choice of how you want to feel about something.

Only if we recognize we are responsible for how we react/respond to everything around us can we not suffer. Pain is a part of life; the suffering is optional (thank you Cheri Huber). But we have to continually (like 500 or 5000 times a day) choose to be in our power and make a choice about how we want to respond. Takes a lot of practice, but so worth it.

Taking our power back always means we are loving ourselves. There is where the real power is, being rooted and grounded, aligned with our Higher Self—that pure, wise, whole loving oversoul which we truly are. And when we are aligned with our Higher Self, simply by being willing, we can make more loving decisions for ourselves, and that is POWERFUL!

Awfulizing

Someone once asked me: "Why is it so hard to be open to the good?"

We wonder what disaster will greet us when we open our email or turn on the news or get a phone call from someone we haven't heard from in a while. It's a very human habit to "awfulize" or "catastrophize." But it's a human creation, which means it's temporary AND we can change our thoughts or perceptions, albeit with a lot of practice.

Life will happen. Bad things will happen. The waves will come. But worrying about things before they happen helps no one and nothing. It's a coping or protective mechanism: if I think the worst, I won't be so upset when it happens. And if something good happens instead, I will be especially relieved or happy.

When we practice being aligned with our Divine nature, we build our reservoir of trust and good feeling. Then we can remember more easily, based on past evidence, that we actually do weather anything that comes our way, even the seemingly impossible things to get through. Since everything is energy and energy is never static, every difficult situation will change at some point. Every feeling will eventually morph into another feeling.

Awfulizing or thinking the worst is a version of "monkey mind" where our mind goes off chattering in a million directions. And it's a practice to stay focused on what we want, not what we don't want. This is where mantras and affirmations come in. Not that the words in and of themselves do anything. But over time, when we are willing to repeat the words with the intent of moving toward the feelings they represent, (all is well, everything is already taken care of perfectly, I am taken care of completely, I cannot be separate from the Universe), they redirect our minds to what we do want (resilience) and away from what we don't want (disaster).

Every time we are willing to say the words of what we would like our experience to be, we are laying in a gossamer wing of good feeling. Lay in enough gossamer wings (that we can't feel as we are laying them in, as they are gossamer) and we will reach critical mass, the 51 percent, and all of a sudden, we will actually FEEL that all is well! No matter what it looks like in the moment.

For years, my mantra has been, "I'm all taken care of. Everything is already done perfectly, better than I can imagine." When I'm really fearful, I repeat them over and over and over— sometimes hundreds of times a day. Eventually I am moved to the feeling of trust, even before I see the result. I trust, I believe before I see, because I have past proof. This is one advantage of getting older: I have a lot of history that I truly am taken care of, and often in seemingly impossible situations. Everything changes. Energy always moves.

It's no different from knitting, teaching, writing, nursing, building. Whatever you are good at took practice and time. This is just another practice. You have your whole lifetime to practice. That is what a lifetime is for. Enjoy the adventure!

Send an SOS to the Universe

The waves of energy can sometimes be very challenging, crashing rather than flowing around us. We, or someone close to us, may experience extreme distress during such times. Something in our human lives causes us to be very troubled. We need a job. We want resolution to a difficult situation. We need money. We feel suffering or angst in our hearts or minds. We need relief—and we need it NOW! We have a deadline.

Fortunately, the Universe always responds to us.

Everything has to happen in Spirit (the invisible) before a projection, picture or image of the resolution can be made visible in our human world. So, our first go-to would be to address the Universe in no uncertain terms: I need help now! I need to find a job this week! I have rent to pay next week! I am ready for this situation to resolve now! I need to know if I should move/take this apartment/buy/sell this house now! I must find the check I misplaced now! I am/my friend/family member is in dire straits and needs help now! You get the idea.

We send an SOS when we really need help RIGHT NOW—really and truly and absolutely need help right now.

The next very important step is to say: And I receive help now! Thank you!

So, we ask and receive in the same breath. We state with confidence (at least 51 percent!) that, once we have given permission to the Universe to pull out all the stops and put everything together in ways we can't even fathom in response to our SOS, of course we will receive the answer without fail. We ask, we do everything we need to do, we do our part, we let go in confidence, we make space to receive the answer, and we persist in the trust and certainty that everything is being put together to answer our request. We just don't know what the answer will look like.

I have seen this work uncountable times. Sometimes I ask for people, and I teach them to ask for themselves. Sometimes I ask the angels to help immediately. However it feels good to you to ask (and receive) is the best way for you.

The Universe has to respond to us; we are indivisibly connected. We just can't expect the solution to look a certain way. That expectation is our human voice, our ego, interfering. But rest assured, we will receive an answer. And the resolution will be for our highest good.

Shoulding on Ourselves

How many times have you said: I should do this, I should do that, I should exercise more, eat better, sleep more, be kinder? And we all wonder how to do more of what we think we "should do." I say, we have to start where everything comes from—in Spirit. This means using the Love that we are, as part of the All, the Universe, Source, All That Is, God, Spirit. We use the energy that we are. We begin by moving that energy with our thought, our intention. Such as: I am WILLING to take loving care of my body. I LOVE walking. I LOVE going to yoga. I LOVE being kind to myself in every way possible. I LOVE getting all the sleep I need.

Believe it or not, this really works and at just the right time, even though we don't know what that right time is. We might believe it "should" occur at a certain time, or we "should" be motivated to do whatever we think we "should" do. The right time is when we are filled up with enough good feeling that it floats us to do what is for our highest good, and much more effortlessly than forcing ourselves unkindly with "should." Shoulding on ourselves is never loving.

What I love about metaphysics is that it's provable. Try the science experiment. See how engaging the Universe, of which you are an indivisible part, creates a response. Of course, it's not always the response you want or expect (more shoulding, this time on the Universe!), but always a response. But you have to do your part, then let go and make space, make room to receive the completed resolution. It will drop in your lap, if you are 51 percent sure everything is all taken care of. Not without your input, but co-creating with your input. Each of us is but a drop of water in the vast ocean, but the ocean would be less and incomplete without our drop. It takes all of us to be the ocean. We are inter-are, as Thich Nhat Hanh says.

My favorite quote about this power that we are is from Rumi: "You are not a drop in the ocean. You are the entire ocean in a drop."

So many spiritual teachers say that what we are really afraid of is our power. True power is that connection with the Universe. That's where all the love is. That's what we are, our Higher Self. The more we merge with our Higher Self (through willingness and allowing), the more we express the love we are. Therein is true power. Love is the strongest force in the Universe—way more powerful than temporary human, aggressive power that always dissipates eventually.

Every time we are willing about anything, and affirm it, we may not feel it in the moment (and usually don't when we start this process), but we are laying in a gossamer wing of good feeling. Lay in enough gossamer wings, and eventually we reach critical mass, 51 percent. We just need to get to that 51 percent certainty that whatever the current situation we are working with is all taken care of, perfectly. This takes letting go and persisting in the trust. I prefer that thought to patience.

Once we reach the 51 percent—and we may not even know we're there until we see the manifestation—this allows the Universe to give to us what we are ready to receive, whatever is for our highest good. It may not necessarily be what we think "should" happen, but what is just right, whether we know what that is or not. And it's always for our highest good and our benefit, no matter what it looks like.

As Mike Dooley writes in *Notes from the Universe*: "One of my favorite things about time and space is that absolutely NOTHING can ever happen there that can't be seen as a blessing in some wonderful way. Perspective rules."

Grounding or . . . Nearthing

I was guiding a client through a grounding exercise once and while talking about the nurturing, nourishing qualities of the yin earth energy, I accidentally combined earth and nourishing/nurturing and said "nearth." And I thought that is a perfect word to use for grounding: nearthing.

It's always a good time to ground—or nearth—our energy, connecting with the cosmos and the earth, anchoring between them. Our Higher Self and the Universe are the perfect balance of yin and yang. Here on earth in our human condition, we vacillate in the balance of yin and yang, affected by all that is happening around us and within us. Grounding helps us balance and handle the influx of any change, within and without.

A simple grounding technique is to imagine the energies above you in the heavens. Breathe in this swirl of energy through the top of your head. With continued gentle inhales and exhales, breathe it all the way through your body down to your feet, and then exhale the energy down into the heart of the earth. Now, again with gentle inhales and exhales, breathe in the earth energy all the way up through your body. You will be nearthed. The cosmic and earth energies will mix in just the right proportion in your body. You can send it with your intention just to where you need it most in your body. Just a few seconds several times during the day can stabilize and harmonize us.

Lori Furbush, a Qi Gong, meditation and yoga teacher in California, says: "The first step in healing is to ground; to start from where you are. Ground your body on the earth. Ground your mind in your body. Ground your breath and your focus in your lower belly."

Focus is such an important tool. If we cannot focus our mind, we cannot harness the energy we need for healing and for digesting life. Pool all of your energy and resources into experiencing the present moment, through the deep center of your being, and feel the vast possibilities that await your next step.

British poet David Whyte writes:

"Ground is what lies beneath our feet. It is the place where we already stand; a state of recognition, the place or the circumstances to which we belong whether we wish to or not. It is what holds and supports us, but also what we do not want to be true. It is what challenges us, physically or psychologically, irrespective of our hoped-for needs. It is the living, underlying foundation that tells us what we are, where we are, what season we are in and what, no matter what we wish in the abstract, is about to happen in our body; in the world or in the conversation between the two.

"To come to ground is to find a home in circumstances and in the very physical body we inhabit in the midst of those circumstances and, above all, to face the truth, no matter how difficult that truth may be. To come to ground is to begin the courageous conversation, to step into difficulty and by taking that first step, begin the movement through all difficulties, to find the support and foundation that has been beneath our feet all along: a place to step onto, a place on which to stand and a place from which to step."

Just Love

Many years ago, my metaphysics teacher Nick Lentine told me to Just Love. It wasn't what I wanted to hear. How could I "just love" a husband (now ex) who wasn't "making me" happy? Wasn't that his job? As I know now, that is my job; it was never his. Maybe he always knew that and, while neither of us knew how to just love, I see now that my ex was trying to love himself in the best way he knew how. It just didn't feel loving to me. And it was time to take responsibility for my own happiness.

We have relationships for many reasons. One of them is to teach us about Love and loving ourselves. The people who love me the most loved me until I could learn to love myself. When I was at my most despairing, sometimes the only thing that kept me from going off the rails was knowing that these two people saw something in me worth loving. And they knew all of me. I wasn't pulling the wool over their eyes. But they held the duality of my human self and my Divine Self until I opened my eyes to my Divine self and had compassion for my human self. Their love illuminated and reflected that place in me until I could see and experience my true self for myself.

Just Love. It's the most we can do and often the only thing we can do.

Oneness . . . We Can Work It Out

My millennial nephews offer these words of wisdom: We need to listen to each other, remember we are all equal and treat each other with respect, understand we will disagree and be willing to find areas where we do agree.

This is a prescription for life and politics. They are talking about Oneness, not separation. They are talking about Love in practice. I trust we can put this into practice and not have to wait until their generation is finally calling the shots. The only way to heal is love.

Let us take a breath together, in Oneness, with all our differences, in love. The Beatles said it in 1965, and it's true today: We can work it out.

The Light is Coming

We experience less and less sunlight each day from the Summer Solstice in June, the day with the most hours of sunlight, until we reach the day with the least amount of sunlight right before the Winter Solstice occurs in December. You might say that during the last days of fall, we are in the heart of the darkness. Once the Winter Solstice dawns, the light will grow every day and build back up to the Summer Solstice.

Fall is the time of letting go, emptying, releasing, grieving. We are called on to release so many of our attachments and ideas of how we think things should be. For some, it can be a very dark time. However, the light always dawns. Our light, our Higher Self, is always present as part of the Light of All That Is, even if we can't always feel it. Our light will always guide us through the darkness, searing away that which no longer serves us so we take nothing that will weigh us down into the winter season of rest and replenishment. So even in our struggles, we notice waves of uplifting energy, the Light pouring in through the cracks.

Author Joanna Macy says: "The heart that breaks open can contain the whole universe."

In "Anthem," Leonard Cohen sings:

Every heart, every heart to love will come

But like a refugee.

Ring the bells that still can ring

Forget your perfect offering

There is a crack, a crack in everything

That's how the light gets in.

Sometimes the expansion of light can feel painful, as it illuminates what has been hidden, both our shadow and our power. In the breaking down, we find it is the path to the breakthrough.

Wishing you more Love and Light than you can imagine.

In this Moment, All is Well

In my practice, I often ask people to be present with me just for a moment to connect with me and let everything else go. The world is there, waiting for us outside of this moment. I invite you to take the next few seconds and be with me, in Spirit. Ready?

Breathe with me. Focus on being right here with me, in this bit of time, this bit of now. In this moment, right now, focusing together, all is well. If you really fall into this moment, inhabit this moment, everything is OK right in this slice of the now. Right here, right now, nothing else happening but just this connection between you and me and All That Is. And we can feel it, tap into it, touch it, simply by being present, right now in this instant. This is the importance and gift of being willing to be present moment to moment. Just be willing.

In a passage titled "Afraid of the Past and the Future" in Jiddu Krishnamurti's book *Freedom from the Known*, the Indian philosopher writes:

"At the actual moment, as I am sitting here, I am not afraid; I am not afraid in the present, nothing is happening to me, nobody is threatening me or taking anything away from me. But beyond the actual moment there is a deeper layer in the mind that is consciously or unconsciously thinking of what might happen in the future or worrying that something from the past may overtake me. So, I am afraid of the past and the future. I have divided time into the past and the future. Thought steps in, says, 'Be careful it does not happen again,' or 'Be prepared for the future. The future may be dangerous for you. You have got something now but you may lose it. You may die tomorrow; your wife may run away; you may lose your job. You may never become famous. You may be lonely. You want to be quite sure of tomorrow.'"

Remember all is well, all is truly well . . . in this moment.

Life is Good

Sometimes during sessions, I ask people to say out loud, Life is good! I want them to see what it feels like and to gauge how true it feels. Often, people will say at first, eh, not so true. And then I begin to reflect back to them all that I know about them—the changes in their lives, how they've learned to love themselves, the progress they've made. I ask them to open their minds and hearts and really hear and feel how someone else views them.

I ask them to suspend their inner critic for just a few moments. I know that when we feel bad about ourselves or our lives, it often doesn't matter what other people say to us. We can't feel it or take it in. Willingness is the key here. It makes space. It lets in light. It lays in a gossamer wing of good feeling that moves us toward love. And it takes gradual, baby steps. So, what I'm trying to do is encourage people to move bit by bit toward feeling the good in their lives, even while there still might be icky things in places.

On this earth plane, we live the duality of being human and Divine, all at the same time. Life is good even while difficult things are happening. As a good friend of mine points out, we can hold both. Life is not black or white. Life is hard and life is good, all at the same time.

The Buddhist teacher Cheri Huber says it's not the content that's important, it's the process. We might say the details are not important. What this means is we're always learning about love, learning to love ourselves, learning that we are inherently joy. And the tough details of life provide contrast to help us choose for love, no matter what those details are. I have my laundry list, you have yours. What's important is how we handle it, what choices we make, if we choose for love, even if we don't know how in the moment. We must be willing, no matter what's happening around us, no matter what the details are.

Journalist Jen Christensen writes about what the Dalai Lama suggests:

"You Do You . . . First step, work on compassion and start by developing it for yourself. 'Mainly,' he (the Dalai Lama) said, feeling happy is largely about 'your own mental attitude.' If you remain someone who is 'honest, truthful,' about how you feel, you can find happiness 'no matter what [the] surrounding situation.'

"His Holiness is talking in part, about the Buddhist concept of self-compassion. He believes we'd all be happier people if we learned more about our own selves and embraced who we are, flaws and all.

"Which side of ourselves will prevail? When you have compassion for someone, typically that means you are recognizing and validating someone's pain. Psychologists have shown when you do that, you automatically develop feelings of kindness and caring for that person.

You develop concern for their general well-being. Self-compassion, then, is when you are kind, rather than critical, toward yourself, even when you mess up or when you are in some form of emotional pain."

Self-compassion is a form of love. If we open the floodgates of willingness and are especially kind to ourselves, we will all get through the details life is presenting us…all in service of choosing for love, which moves us to joy. No matter what is happening. Life truly IS good.

It's None of Your Business

I love this story. It happened in a group therapy setting. A young man was talking about how people were judging him, what others thought about what he was doing, and how upset he was at what he was sure other people were thinking about him. Someone in the group who seemed to be nodding off suddenly raised his head, looked at the young complaining man and said, "Kid, what other people think of you is none of your business." And he resumed his seeming napping.

Pretty astounding words of wisdom and very true. Simple. But not easy to apply, as usual.

It's very hard not to be affected by other people and what we imagine they think about us. But all that brings us suffering. How wonderful that life has such built-in challenges to help us learn how to stay on our own paths!

All we can ever do is live our own lives. This is the Law of Individuality. We are not meant to be on anyone else's paths (except those of our children, for a time). We don't live anyone else's life path and they can't live ours. When we wander off our path, as all of us are wont to do regularly, we distract ourselves from our own work. That's when we catch ourselves thinking about other people and what they should be doing or what they are thinking about us.

Every time we realize we are thinking about someone else and what they are doing or should be doing, or telling ourselves a story about what someone else is thinking about us, we can practice catching ourselves. Then we can forgive ourselves for getting off our path temporarily and get back on it, with our intention. Of course, our human mind wants to distract us! Our human mind finds great difficulty in being present with just ourselves and thinking about what is most loving to us in the moment. That would be boring, selfish and uncomfortable, or so our human mind tells us. So much more interesting to think about someone else's path. And so much less fulfilling and nourishing. When we choose to be on our path and align with our Higher Self and fill up with all the good feeling and love we are, then we can spill that over to everyone and everything around us.

Of course, when we stay on our own paths, take loving care of ourselves and release excessive responsibility for others (by not getting on their paths), not everyone is happy. If another is not taking loving care of themselves, they may not be too happy that we are. When we relinquish (false) responsibility for someone else, they may not like that they are left to stew on their path because they don't know they are completely taken care of, as we all are. Just not always the way we would like to be or think it should be. Therein is the danger and suffering of being attached to how we think it should be.

I wish you the strength to stay on your path, so as to find the joy in you and in your life.

Keeping to Your Own Path

And just how do we stay on our path and mind our own business?

This is something I think about and apply every day, all through the day. I've concluded that it's simple, but not easy. I try to keep things uncomplicated and efficient so every day, before I get out of bed, or into the shower, I imagine my Higher Self. Currently she looks like a swirl of purple and gold. (Your Higher Self can also be a sound or a symbol, or whatever comes to mind.) Then I breathe her in, every day, all through the day, whenever I think of it, or whenever I don't feel harmonious. She is my pure wisdom, highest integrity, she is the love, peace and harmony that I am, my eternal self. I state that I love seeing through her eyes, hearing through her ears, speaking through her mouth, loving through her heart. She is the peace and love that I AM.

Then every time I feel discordant or angry or frustrated or human in any of our usual ways, I think of her/me and breathe her in. If I start thinking of someone else and what they should be doing or questioning why they are doing what they are doing, as soon as I catch it (which is easier and easier because I feel the interruption of good feeling when I get off my path, when I am not present, which tells me I am not connected to my Higher Self), I forgive myself for getting on someone else's path and off mine (over and over and over during the day) and put myself back on my path. It can be very uncomfortable at first. But when we look within, our paths have many unexplored places!

We just haven't known or given ourselves permission that it's OK to be self-focused on self-care. But when we do focus on self-care, connecting with our Higher Self, we fill ourselves up with the love and good feeling that we inherently are. By being focused on the present, we get the signals in our body and mind when we are not in alignment with the Love that we naturally are. And each time, when we forgive ourselves for whatever we are doing that is not creating good feeling, we connect back to our Higher Self (which can never really be separate from us anyway, but we open up the door again and again), and that good feeling fills us up and spills over and floats us to where we need to go or what we need to do. Truly, all we need to do is be willing to focus on being present on our path and in tune with our Higher Self and restoring good feeling and the rest is taken of, organically and naturally. Simple, not easy.

It just takes willingness (the key) and awareness of what we are thinking. Fortunately, the effects of what we are thinking show up in our bodies and lives, so even if we're not aware, we can feel what's going on, then forgive ourselves and make corrections. Because stepping off our path, out of alignment with our higher selves, feels bad. Thankfully! There's a blessing in everything, even getting out of alignment with the peace and love we are. It shows us how powerful we are. And then, in that awareness, we can make a choice.

So, another mantra I say every day is: I release whatever I might be holding onto that might be blocking my flow of good feeling (my connection to my Higher Self), even if I have no idea what I might be holding onto. And I receive gratefully whatever is for my highest good— more good than I can imagine—by making space and releasing in trust.

My wish for all of you is to feel the Love that you ARE. It's the best! And we go in and out of the awareness and feeling because we are both human and Divine. And it's all good.

The Freedom of Not Knowing

When we stay on our own path, feeling our connection with our Higher Self which is evident by our feeling good, we are also in a "don't know mind" about everyone else. Speaking as a former know-it-all, I can tell you it is very freeing to say, I don't know.

I used to think that I always knew the best way to do something. As I matured, I discovered that, lo and behold, other people actually had really good ideas too! Just different from mine and often better. Imagine, there was a good or better way to do something other than my way!

When we don't know, we are open to possibilities. We don't have to figure everything out. We create space for unknown—and maybe better than we can imagine—solutions to flow in. And it's a very good way to get off everyone else's path and back on our own. If someone asks you what you think about someone else or what they're doing or why they're doing what they're doing, you can't really know anything about that person's motivations or what they're thinking. You're not living in their mind or their life. Much easier to say you don't know!

All we can change is our own mind and our life. When we realize we don't know a lot of things, and we don't know anything about anyone else for sure, and we remember that our true work is to circulate love and good feeling to ourselves first, everything gets simpler. Then we refocus on self-care, which requires us to be on our path, paying attention to what's going on in our life and our body and our mind. That's a job in and of itself. And the best adventure in the world. Because then we fill up with all that love and good feeling which in turn spills over. And that allows us to give from a full vessel.

I love this quote from American author and astrologer Rob Brezsny:

"'I don't know' is an unparalleled source of power, a declaration of independence from the pressure to have an opinion about every single subject. It's fun to say. Try it: 'I don't know.' Let go of the drive to have it all figured out: 'I don't know.' Proclaim the only truth you can be totally sure of: 'I don't know.' Empty your mind and lift your heart: 'I don't know.' Use it as a battle cry, a joyous affirmation of your oneness with the Great Mystery: 'I don't know.'"

The Joy of Mercury Retrograde

Retrograde periods occur when a planet appears to be going backwards in its orbit. It's often a time where old issues come up for review, reassessment and release. Think of the "re" in the word retrograde which means again, or redo.

We often associate Mercury retrograde with electronic or mechanical malfunctions or communication misfires or glitches. To understand what retrograde means for us, think of some words that begin with "re." Revisiting, reinventing, reassessing, review, release, renew, reconcile. For me, times of Mercury retrograde often mean revisiting old patterns, particularly my old familiar friends overwhelm and pressure. What I do with all the old baggage that shows itself once again is to recognize it as old remnants of energy, breathe into the present moment and check in with what is actually happening right here and now. I'm then willing to release the old energy with a sense of kindness and compassion for myself. No matter what old pattern or way of thinking or behaving arises, we recognize and we release, with love, focusing on what is really true about the present moment.

Remember, things rise up for resolution when we are filled up enough with good feeling to handle that rising up. Then we can use all of that good feeling that we have built up in our moat or reservoir to surround that old pattern in love. We have infinite capacity to love because our Higher Self is infinite Love. In our human form, we usually don't remember this essential truth.

Every year, my bountiful irises remember how to bloom and every year they multiply and are more beautiful. They know and fulfill their infinite capacity without even thinking. I aspire to be like my irises and rise up every year even more joyfully than the year before. I wish you the same.

Take a Breath, Make a Choice

I was walking on our greenway one summer morning, inhaling the intoxicating scent of the honeysuckle, and ran into a lovely friend walking her lovely dog. We exchanged news and pleasantries about friends and blessings, and blessings in disguise. We briefly talked about family and how everyone was doing. And we talked about the changes everyone was going through. We circled back to no matter how things change, life is still good in this moment—that in this very moment there is something to feel grateful for, something about which to circulate good feeling.

When we make the choice to really sink into this present moment, we can ask, is everything all right this immediate moment? In this right-now moment, we can say everything is good in this tiny space, in this little sliver of now. Even with life swirling all around us.

We always have a choice no matter what we are thinking about or how we are thinking. One Buddhist teacher says that one way to embrace what is actually happening in life is simply to say: Oh, this is what is happening now! Whether we are trying to lose weight or deal with anxiety or things are falling apart, at some point we make a choice to notice life is happening. But what is really happening right now? Am I OK? We do this over and over and over again.

Metaphysician and author Louise Hay says the power is in the present moment. That's where we notice and make a choice. And what is the choice? Whatever feels most loving to us, whatever will kindly and tenderly take care of us. It takes practice. Human life gives us lots of practice!

We take a breath, we make a loving choice.

We do this until we build up those gossamer layers of good feeling and crest over the 51 percent threshold of good feeling. We may not even know how close to the 51 percent we are until we realize life feels better, and even good, no matter what is happening.

The Right Time

To every thing there is a season, and a time to every purpose
under the heaven: A time to be born, and a time to die. . .

— Ecclesiastes 3:1 (KJV)

This is a very familiar scripture to many of us although I have to admit, I first became aware of it listening to the Byrds' 1965 tune, "Turn! Turn! Turn!" My scriptural education was a bit lacking. But for everything, there is a right time.

As humans, we sometimes think we know the right time. During her last days, a very dear friend of mine, and a very spiritual being full of light, would say, "I don't know why I'm still here. I'm ready!" And then we would say what we both knew to be the truth: that she would cross over at the right time and Perfect Intelligence knew when that was. While we are an indivisible part of All That Is, we are still human and see through our human filters and desires. The right time may be something different from what we think.

When I first thought of writing this column, bits and pieces of what I wanted to say kept coming to me and I wanted to sit down and just get it done. But it wasn't the right time. Maybe I want to finish some website work, some computer work, some bookkeeping, some ironing, some housecleaning, some gardening. And, in being kind and loving and compassionate to me, I ask: Is it the right time? Maybe it's the right time to sit and talk and laugh with my best friend, watch a movie with my husband, cuddle with our kitty, take a nap, read a book, do some yoga stretches, or relax with a glass of wine. And maybe it's time to clean the bathroom!

When I check in with my Higher Self, that perfectly aware part of me that sees the whole picture, and trust and honor my true self, then I stop pushing the river, stop pushing myself. And everything gets done, in its right time. Easily, effortlessly.

Your Right Path to a Healthy Body

There is a right time for everything and that includes taking steps to improve our health. There's a right time to lose weight and begin right movement, whether that be yoga, walking or working out. And if we push ourselves before it's time, we can become frustrated if we don't accomplish what we want or if we can't stick to our plan/expectations/ program/diet. So, what can we do?

Since everything begins in Spirit, and actually has to come to completion in Spirit before we see it in the visible, in our lives, we have to start in Mind, in Spirit, which means working with our Higher Self. How do we do that?

One of the keys to healing (along with love) is willingness. We simply state to ourselves something like this: I am willing to move my body in the right way. I am willing to lovingly take care of my body in how I eat and how I move. I am willing to see the expression of my Higher Self in my body and my life. I am willing to let go of my resistance to taking loving care of myself. I am willing to love myself more than I can imagine. We decide what words resonate with us; we will know what feels right.

As with any affirmation, it isn't the words that make the difference. We use the words to bring ourselves to the feeling. And we must be at least 51 percent at the feeling of being willing to take loving care of ourselves. That allows the picture of what we want to actually appear in our body and our life. That allows the idea in Spirit, the desire, to complete and migrate into our life experience. And remember, we are working toward the 51 percent. We are still human beings, as well as spiritual beings, and we must have compassion for our humanity. We are not going to be perfect and we are not meant to be perfect in our human counterpart. Yes, our spiritual self is whole, perfect and complete, which is why we want to be willing to have that loving energy flow into our bodies and into our lives unimpeded, but it's not going to happen 100 percent, because we are still in human form. So, we need to have compassion for the condition of being human!

I have used this technique over the years for so much of my healing—when I wanted to start to walk more regularly, go back to yoga, pay more attention to my nutrition, rest more, lose weight. We can look at the Pillars of Health: right rest, right nutrition, right movement, right relationship within and without. We can be willing to hear which pillar is most important right now. When I ask people the question of which pillar really feels like the one they need to attend at the present time, they are often surprised at the answer their Higher Self gives them, but it is always true. And then we work with that, willingly and trusting in the process.

And over the years I actually have become more loving to myself. I do yoga regularly, walk regularly, sleep more, eat what feels most loving to me and have lost 60 pounds. None of it happened quickly. I must have been willing to walk for two months before I started to do it. I had yoga in my mind for months before I began taking a class. I was nearly 60 when the weight started coming off, about a pound a week, after being overweight for many years.

The Universe heard my desire and answered me, easily, effortlessly, conveniently, and at just the right time. I had to do my part. As I filled up with love and compassion for myself, it spilled over into expression, in just the right way, at just the right time. I am continually in wonder and awe at the Perfect Intelligence of which we are a part.

Abundance

Consider the Summer Solstice, the day of the year with the most hours of sunlight. It's a time of not only abundant sunlight, but abundant lushness, abundant rain, abundant heat. And it's a reminder that natural abundance is always all around us. So why do we often feel lack? When we feel lack, we feel separate from the natural abundance that is too, well, abundant to ignore!

So, a simple fix (but perhaps not an easy one) would be to give up the idea, the feeling of separation from all that undeniable abundance and claim our rightful experience as one of abundance. Since everything springs from one Source, if there is abundance somewhere, there must be abundance everywhere. The trick is to allow the natural flow of abundance from Source into our lives. One way to allow this is to cultivate and be willing to experience an abundance of good feeling, about anything! Since we live in a visible, human world, there will be a manifestation of what we feel 51 percent of the time (whether it's true or not). So, if we feel lack or we focus on limitation and restriction, we will experience that in some way. If we are willing to feel flowing, abundant good feeling at least 51 percent of the time, we will experience and see a corresponding picture of that abundant good feeling.

I like to stop at times and remember what there is to feel good about in my life. I feel good about visits from dear friends. I'm grateful when our garden is weeded and cleaned up and for the hardworking young men from our neighborhood who help keep it that way. They exemplify all that is good about the younger generation, and make me very grateful that I don't have to do it all myself! I'm happy when I get a stay-cation; I rejoice at having time off and spending time at home. And I always know I will feel good going back to the office and seeing people I love and love to work with.

I always send out a thank you when I see repeating numbers, especially 1:11 or 11:11 on digital clocks and know my angels and guides are letting me know that I'm taken care of and held in love. (The Universe finds electronics an easy way to communicate with us!) I'm always abundantly grateful my car is running. I revel in spending time with my family in my comfortable home. I love all the green surrounding me here in North Carolina, especially considering I come originally from dry Southern California, which can often be desert-like.

I marvel at how our kitty came to us and has enriched our lives and is the perfect little being for us, like all our four-legged family members have been. I feel my heart opening ever more as the abundant unconditional love that animals naturally are flow into our lives.

And sometimes I have the best time cooking. I love that I can have so much fun preparing simple food and I love how good that food tastes. And I am so appreciative of my kitchen appliances. I routinely bless the washer and dryer, too.

Life lives through us, and we can just say YES!

Finding Your Rhythm

When we are willing to take loving care of ourselves, we are more able to find our true rhythm. This is something I've been mulling over for some time. When I was diagnosed with cancer, I cut back my schedule somewhat, but kept working through two surgeries and six weeks of radiation, taking only a few days off. It felt like it was the right thing to do at the time, as I was used to keeping very busy. That seemed like my natural rhythm.

But over time, I began to question that. I always planned a lot, thought a lot, scheduled a lot, and did a lot. But to whose rhythm was I moving? Was this who I really was, my authentic self, or was I acting on ideas about who I was supposed to be that I had adopted or internalized?

Bit by bit, since all progress is in baby steps, I became willing to know what my natural rhythm was now. I noticed I was happier working less, connecting with family and friends more, sleeping more, paying more attention to what proper nutrition meant now, what kind of exercise felt right, how much down time felt good, how much alone time I needed. It felt good to be more discerning and aware of what felt good and what didn't. I kept asking myself, what's the most loving thing I can do right now?

It took a long time to unloose the ties that bound me to past messages, the "shoulds" of what needed to get done before I could allow myself to veg out, relax, watch a movie, read, or just be. I finally decided that it didn't matter if how I used to be was my natural rhythm or someone else's that got imposed on me; what was important was that when it was no longer serving me, I chose differently.

When we are aware, we can make a choice. And in that awareness, we can also keep evolving and refining.

Take loving care of yourself and listen for your own rhythm.

Just Show Up

After the historic solar eclipse of Aug. 21, 2017, and during the last week of Mercury retrograde (which ended on Sept. 5), it seemed there was no end to our individual and collective crises, issues, and old patterns. In my case, one family member experienced a broken elbow, five days in intensive care and surgery that would take three months to heal. I knew of people who lost jobs, needed major surgery, had loved ones going into nursing homes, were involved in car accidents—all in addition to the usual day-to-day challenges.

And in the weeks that followed, people recovered from major unexpected surgery and went back to work. Caregivers were finally given respite. Art spaces opened up to be filled with joyous new creations. Jobs were found. People fell in love with new grandchildren. Our energy was finally restored.

It's all energy so it all changes eventually, no matter how dire things may seem at the moment. And since life only moves toward the good, it truly is all moving toward more good, no matter what it looks like now. And it's all a mystery. We never know what's around the corner. So, what do we do with all this? What do we do with life that is happening while we are in the midst of making other plans?

We just show up, every day. Every day we say, so this is what's happening today! And we are willing to feel, bit by bit, gossamer wing by gossamer wing, what we may not see but what we trust. And we trust that we are connected to all that is Love, that all is completely taken care of already, that all is well. And we can't wait to see how it all unfolds, always for our highest good.

The 51 Percent Solution

Sherlock Holmes' panacea may have been a seven percent solution, but anyone who spends any time with me knows about the 51 percent. We are human and Divine all at the same time, and we might as well give up ever being 100 percent because we are partly both. We just strive to be 51 percent aligned with our Divine being and to be willing to embrace the rest of how we are at any given moment.

We all have times that are very challenging where things just do not seem to go smoothly in some regards but all is good and loving in other ways. We struggle to find that place of peace in heart and mind, knowing and feeling when we are just shy of the 51 percent. We may step over that threshold, where our hearts soften and open and we know and feel that all is well and that we are completely taken care of, only to slip under the wire again.

At times like these, knowing I am part of the whole, part of All That Is, that my true nature, my Higher Self, is loving, peaceful, abundant in everything I could need, I ask my angels and guides for help. I imagine my Higher Self and merge with her. I allow myself to be infused with the loving energy I always am, but my human self sometimes forgets.

And I speak silently to the higher selves of those involved in my issues, and give up whatever I am holding onto that feels glitchy and unsmooth. I surrender all I am doing to interrupt my flow of good feeling and ask for help. I receive it and I let go.

When I'm over the 51 percent, I feel the peace and equanimity of my true self. Life may still be messy. Some things may still need to be resolved. But I can feel the shift.

How does the shift into the 51 percent happen? It's always the same, no matter what the details are. I am just willing: willing to be uncomfortable, willing to embrace all that is going on, willing to be sad, willing to be wherever I am, willing to surrender whatever I am holding onto, willing to ask for and receive help and guidance, and willing to trust in that process to bring me into alignment with the flow of peace and love that I inherently am.

Yogi Bhajan said: "If you want to learn something, read about it. If you want to understand something, write about it. If you want to master something, teach it."

This is why I teach about the 51 percent and Love. And I know it will be a lifelong journey.

A Time to Let Go

Fall is a time to gather, to harvest what we have grown, understood and resolved during the summer. As the energy begins to contract in the yin of autumn, we keep what will sustain us in the coming quieter, darker time of hibernation and re-nourishment, and let go of what no longer serves us.

In Chinese Medicine, fall is thought of as the time of letting go, and making room to let come what we need to sustain us through the next season of yin before the yang of spring. It is the time of the metal element, a time of restructuring, tearing down what doesn't support us, so our new, stronger infrastructure can begin to be planned and eventually built.

I love fall and winter. I love the internal times. It's the perfect time to simply affirm: I let go of whatever I need to release. I make room to receive whatever is for my highest good.

We let go, we let come. We don't have to worry about the how or the details. We will be guided as to what our part is. We stay willing. We trust.

Louise Hay, who died in August of 2017 at the age of 90, was a master metaphysician and her books are a mainstay of modern metaphysics. I first read her "I Love Myself" prayer/affirmation more than 30 years ago. I have read this and given it out uncountable times. It always moves me and touches my heart. Here is the end of it:

"I love myself; therefore, I forgive and totally release the past experiences and I am free.

I love myself; therefore, I live totally in the now, experiencing each moment as good and knowing that my future is bright and joyous and secure, for I am a beloved child of the Universe and the Universe lovingly takes care of me now and forever more. And so it is."

Little Deaths

I think about death a lot, although not in a morbid, fearful way. I started this ruminating about death because as child, I had a gut-wrenching, panic attack level fear of death. Now I think about death more in a continuous, letting go sort of way. I call these "little deaths."

Little deaths can be letting go of people, jobs, identities. When I stopped thinking of myself as someone who did certain things, even if it was something I was good at or had dreamed of or enjoyed but my heart no longer sang while doing it (like riding and owning motorcycles), that was a little death. Leaving a marriage, even if it was the most loving thing to do for me and ultimately for the person I no longer loved in the same way, was another little death. Still more little deaths involved giving up the ideas of where I might travel to, or what I needed to accomplish in my life. Not that I was necessarily sad about all these things; it was just time to let go.

I find great truth in the old saw: Friendships (or relationships) are for a reason, a season, or forever. Relationships all have a natural lifespan, whether it's with a person, or with the things I can't imagine letting go of—until I can and I do. The energy I was holding around the person or thing changed. I was no longer nourished in some way and it was time to send the energy into the stream of life for someone else to enjoy.

Sometimes our ego has a little death. Sometimes our human voice (more than our inner wisdom) is holding us together, telling us who we are or who we were expected to be. Sometimes the voice belongs to someone else, like a parent. And sometimes it's our voice, although not our true, authentic voice. And at various times in our life, our spirit, our Higher Self, says, I am ready for more good than this. I am ready to take a leap.

Then everything starts to shimmer, move. And instead of saying, I trust this, this is what I asked for, enjoy the ride, I can't wait to see where this takes me, we became fearful and insecure. We ask, what does this mean if I let go of who I know myself to be, in whom I've spent considerable time and effort, what will I be? Maybe I should hold on to what I know. I am fearful of the unknown.

And in fear, we might try to hold on to energy to stop or slow the forward progression of illumination or unfoldment. But this is an illusion. We can't stop the forward movement of energy. We might get depressed or anxious as we depress and deny where our Spirit wants to move. Our true voice, Divine spark, says, this is not our natural state of joy and harmony, this is unnatural, unreal. And eventually we say out loud or silently: This isn't working! I need help! I need another way of thinking or relating or understanding.

This may come in baby steps. We let go, gradually, of how we do something, or think of something, or how we treat ourselves or others. We continue on our journey of truth and unfolding the good and become willing to take the leap into the unseen—in baby steps, usually. And we move into more love, deeper experience, living a life of more connection and deeper communication.

All of this is a trial run for our so-called "death." As we go through these cycles in our life, removing layer after layer, we feel more acutely because we are more naked, more vulnerable. Living a mindful life, perhaps we are more able to have a mindful, "good" death, to make a seamless transition, because we have gotten down to the last layers and we joyfully let them go, finally. We experience our being as so light and effervescent. And then, willingly, happily and with great gratitude for how it has served us and been our partner, we release our body and rejoin Spirit, return home.

So, I'm happy for all my little deaths, the rehearsal for the big kahuna none of us escape.

Be Light

Be the change that you wish to see in the world.

— Mahatma Gandhi

I have always loved this quote, and always wrestled with how to apply it in my life. When I lost two friends in fires in Santa Rosa, Calif., in October of 2017, it really came home to me. Many more friends were displaced by the fires and those friends had many friends who lost their homes. The sadness was overwhelming. The smoke in my mind's eye came not just from the natural disaster in my old hometown and others around the country, but also from the divisiveness that had settled on our country at the time, which felt just as sad to me.

How could I cut through this heaviness and be the change I wished to see in the world? How could I be Light and Love? As usual, the simplest answer was the best. We simply Be Light, Be Love. And we do that by imagining.

We imagine we are a point of light, a flow, a pillar of light and of love. We imagine what is always true (even if we can't feel it): that we are always an indivisible part of the flow of loving light. We receive it. We fill up with that infinite flow from Source, and spill it over to everyone and everything. I imagine pink clouds of love flowing through me and out to every troubled place and person in the world. I do this daily. I persist in being the Light and Love I wish to see in the world. And since everything circles around in this Universe, I know all that love returns to me multiplied. It's important that I receive it to complete the circle, fill up even more, and send that expanded love and light out again.

I remember reading a story long ago about an angel who took a despairing human being above the earth. The human being looked down and saw countless points of light beaming from all over the planet.

"What are all those lights?" the human asked the angel.

"Those are all the prayers and loving thoughts emanating from people around the earth to each other," the angel answered.

And the human realized there was always Love and Light being offered from somewhere in the Universe. We only need to receive and then we, too, can be and feel the Light and Love for ourselves and others once again. We can remind those who have forgotten their light.

We are all Light and Love. Fill up with it and spill it over to everyone and everywhere in our beautiful and struggling world.

The Light Wave of 2017

It seemed that 2017 flew by. During the year, we experienced the accelerated wave of light that actually began pouring into this earth plane in the 1950s and got pumped up in the 1960s leading to the Flower Children, Summer of Love and the Counterculture Movement. Then the Harmonic Convergence in August of 1987 opened up more energetic portals. Many lightworkers were working in Spirit to strengthen the crystalline grid that surrounds the earth so the energy field of the earth would be strong enough to begin absorbing and utilizing the powerful waves of energy. Those waves kept increasing until 2012 when many intuitives and energy workers, and others in tune with the flows of energy, received messages and felt the shift coming. And high frequency, high vibration waves of light and love began pouring in earnest into the earth plane—and into us.

We were being gently encouraged to let go of what was not in alignment with this high integrity energy and open to the Love we are. We were being nudged into understanding we truly are an indivisible part of Spirit, part of the flow of love that is Universal Life Force Energy, and surrendering anything unlike love. Each year since 2012 the clarion call became more insistent, louder, until 2017 when the waves of light illuminated things long held secret, hidden, exposed to the light old patterns that need to be changed, and will be changed, in this powerful surge of light. No holds barred anymore, no more excuses. This is occurring on both the world stage, the macrocosm, and our individual stages, our lives, our microcosms.

December of 2017 was even more illuminating as we moved through the darkest days of the year, the days with the least hours of light, in the run up to the Winter Solstice. The wheel turns on the Solstice and we begin to have more light each day, culminating on the day with the most hours of light, the Summer Solstice. A perfect metaphor for life, the darkness and light, but always moving toward more light, more good, inevitably.

Please join me in surrendering all that is unlike love in our lives, our hearts and our world, and joyfully ride the tide of light into more good and more love than we can imagine.

Rest

Having a lot of time off is a recurring fantasy of mine. I stay home and I get everything done around the house that I never seem to have time to do—or don't make time to do. But on the rare occasions that I do have ample time off, I usually don't attend to housework or much of anything for that matter. It turns out that during those times, what I need to do is just rest.

I sometimes talk about the "do be do be do" principle (thank you Dan Dan the Rainbow Man and Frank Sinatra) which means we need to do some, be some, do some, be some. Our society and our world encourage "doing" all the time; "being" is not a valuable commodity. After all, what are we accomplishing by just being? And thus, we miss the point.

We need to be in order to do. We need to fall silent, rest, zone out, do nothing, loll around on the couch, or daydream in order to fill up our reservoir so we have the energy and enthusiasm to do. We always worry that if we are tired and need to rest, we are lazy or we'll never get ourselves together to do what needs to be done.

I've learned that I often don't need to get done the things I think I need (or want) to do, certainly not in the very moment I think I need to do them. And if I push through the tiredness, I just feel terrible. Sometimes we are tired or low energy because we are processing old energy, and we need to give ourselves the time and space to do that, or the old energy weighs on us and eventually hinders our health. I have experienced this a number of times. I feel the need to take a break or rest, I resist, I get sick. I didn't honor what my inner being was trying to tell me, trying to get me to hear and feel, through the signal of the tiredness. But my stubborn human mind can be very obstinate, very hard-headed. You'd think I'd learn! But that is what we have a lifetime for. Eventually we learn to listen to our higher selves—our true wisdom, our integrity, the Love we are—and act on that love more than we ignore it.

There are times when I need to rest and take it easy that I can almost feel the energetic gears grinding away and I know that is the work I need to allow at the moment. I don't need to know what is processing or what I'm moving through. I just need to trust my inner intelligence which is indivisible from all loving intelligence. What I know now is that if I trust it out (one could say, if I am patient, although I prefer trusting it out!), I will eventually move through it (at just the right time!). And my resting clears the way for regeneration and rejuvenation, and allows me to fill up so I then can do what is appropriate—which may not be what I would like to do or think I need to do.

I remember once taking a little vacation to spend time with a friend. We just stayed home and tooled around locally. We had no agenda, only a few plans that could easily be changed. I slept in and generally took it easy.

Often when we are ready to take time off, we are on our last leg of our energy, so to speak, and desperate for a break. We can't wait for that last day to be over. When this vacation started for me, I was almost surprised it was here. I hadn't drained my energy supply. I was fairly filled up and almost felt like I didn't need the time off that was planned.

What does it feel like to be really filled up? We think we are nourished, rested, we feel pretty good. Then we really get a rest, really get a chance to refill our reservoir and refuel our energy. That's when we fully realize what it means to feel filled up.

When I returned to the office at the end of the vacation, I noticed I was excited to see clients, happy to be doing Reiki/Acupressure sessions, looking forward to all the details of my practice. I was glad to be back at "work," which didn't feel like work at all! And I realized that I was really rested and filled up! This felt markedly different from what I usually would think of as filled up.

Listen to your inner wisdom and you will know when to do and when to be.

The Pillars of Health

Finding ways to take loving care of ourselves may not be as obvious as we think. When I was diagnosed with cancer, I had to stop, take a breath, think about the treatment (two surgeries and radiation) and then ask myself: How do I need to take loving care of myself? As always, I considered the Pillars of Health.

Indian-born physician and author Deepak Chopra recommends five pillars to consider:

Sleep: Aim for seven to eight hours of good quality sleep every night.

Meditation: Spend time every day in silence, reconnecting with your inner self.

Exercise: Move your body every day by walking, doing simple yogic stretching or weight training.

Emotions: Be aware of your relationships; are they supporting your spiritual goals?

Nutrition: Eat healthy, fresh foods with a focus on fruits and vegetables.

Grounding: Stay connected to Mother Earth; spend time in nature.

My recommendations are simpler:

Right rest

Right nutrition

Right movement

Right relationship, within and without

Each of these pillars means whatever is right for you. Only you know how much rest you need, what kind of movement and nutrition resonates with you, and how you need to work on your relationship with your Higher Self and Spirit, and with the people in the world around you.

So, after my diagnosis, I sat quietly, connected within, and asked which pillar of health was most important for me at the moment. What would support me the most? What did I need the most? And the answer was right in front of me: right rest. And, thus, I found out how much rest I needed. Over the next year and a half, I slept, and slept and slept, sometimes 10-plus hours a day. I thought it might take a year to "rest enough," but my rest changed for good. I never realized how much rest I needed, and never gave myself enough.

At some point, I felt rested, so I asked within what pillar I needed to consider next. And nutrition was the answer. Then movement. Of course, all along we are working on right relationship. We actually work on each pillar in degrees most of the time. But if you ask what is most loving for you right now, you might be surprised at the answer.

We have all our answers within, if we will only ask. And listen. What does your inner voice say right now about which pillar of health needs some loving attention?

Dust Bunnies

Maybe you've noticed it too. Since we're all part of the Collective One Mind, we often experience similar things at the same time. The dust bunnies have been coming out of the corners. These are just remnants of energy, of old stuff, that we've already processed, looked at, analyzed, and released for the most part.

The waves of high frequency, loving energy that are pouring into the earth plane are whipping up the bits and pieces, the leftovers, and bringing them into view—not for us to do anything about, but just for us to notice and let go of. We've done a lot of work around these old issues. These are just the scraps of energy, the last debris just coming up to be released. The dust bunnies. We don't need to examine them or take them apart, just sweep them away.

I've noticed thoughts and memories about old relationships, my old patterns of behavior, long ago situations, stuff I haven't thought about in years, just rising up, odds and ends. And it's just giving me an opportunity to feel the love I am now, and surround the person I was then in love.

Everything is an expression of love or a call for love. So, don't get too involved in your dust bunnies. Just lovingly gather them up, know they once served you and are now ready to be released to the light of love and transformation.

It's OK to Be Uncomfortable

When we rest, when we make space, when we let go, it doesn't always feel blissful. Nirvana does not automatically follow. Meditation isn't always comfortable or joyous or enlightening. Slowing down and allowing ourselves to be more present opens us to the light—our light—and sometimes that light illuminates things we are holding that we need to be aware of so we can make a choice about what to do with them. Sometimes the light illuminates the dust bunnies, those remnants of energy that just need to be released.

This process is not necessarily comfortable. And when something is uncomfortable, we tend to shy away from it, judge it, and say to ourselves: Well, if it doesn't feel good, it's not what I want to go through.

Transition is uncomfortable. But it's OK if something we are trying on for size feels awkward at first. We'll get through it.

When we first practice a new behavior, that's just what it is, new and unpracticed. It takes time for us to get good at something whether it's playing the piano, writing, teaching, using new styles of communication or taking loving care of ourselves. It can be somewhat painful and we might be tempted to give it up. But that's just part of the process.

So, when we feel uncomfortable as we try on new, more loving behavior, or when we practice taking better care of ourselves, we can be kind to ourselves, take time to breathe, and be willing to trust out the process. We can be willing to sit with the edginess that might be going on and embrace all of it. Life includes all of everything! We can practice tolerance for the distress we feel as we experience the newness of giving ourselves space or love or kindness.

It's OK if we are temporarily uncomfortable as we get used to and apply the Love we truly are. That same Love surrounds and supports us, holds us and is completely at ease waiting for us to catch up to its truth.

Navigating by Crisis

Life is messy, awkward, uncomfortable. We try to have a Plan B (or C or D). We try to think of every possible scenario. We think we will feel better if only we can control situations and people, if only they would just listen to us! Because after all, we know what's best. (I used to think like this all the time.) Then, as the saying goes, life happens as we are making other plans.

When we are in a roller coaster situation of any kind, where one thing after another is happening and all our best-laid plans are going awry, that's when we wind up navigating by crisis. Or we try to plan for every eventuality and the thing we never would have thought would happen, happens.

Sometimes everything in the world and our own lives seems so intense that it feels like we are careening from one crisis to another. I felt this way during the last years of my mother's life.

I had no idea how I was going to manage everything, including her resistance to having more help or eventually being in a nursing home. I just kept telling her: It's all taken care of. It will all get figured out. I don't know how, but it's all taken care of already.

Of course, I was terrified inside, and had no idea how it would all be taken care of, but I had no other option than to trust. And when my mom would get scared, she would say to me, "It's all taken care of, right?" And I'd tell her it was, mostly because I had no other answer. And that helped manage my own fear.

When her health situation spiraled out of control and crisis after crisis began occurring, in the midst of everything, we navigated. Responding to each crisis and each symptom, we let ourselves be guided and directed by what was happening in the present moment. Everything was coming too fast to handle any other way than moment to moment and step by step.

I certainly didn't do everything perfectly, but I did the best I could. I navigated by crisis. Maybe it looked like I was lurching from one decision or issue to the next, but that was the way I had to navigate right then. And indeed, it all worked out. She and I were all taken care of in ways we couldn't have imagined and, ultimately, we saw that it was for her highest good and that of all concerned. No matter what it looked like along the way.

Letting Go

The end of the year is a natural time of reflection. It's a time when I think: What did I learn during these past 12 months? At the end of 2017, the answer came to me right away. I learned to let go.

We can call it surrendering, allowing, releasing. I just think of it as letting go. Letting go of everything that is in the way of connecting to my Higher Self. Letting go of everything that is in the way of feeling the Love that I am. Letting go of everything that is unlike Love. Letting go of everything that keeps me from being present, from being kind to myself. Letting go of what is overwhelming me, what stresses me, what confuses me, what frustrates me, what angers me. I just let go. I don't have to know what any of it is. I can feel it. I just let go.

In just letting go, we make space. We make room. There is a possibility of something else, something other than whatever we are suffering at the moment. There is the possibility of ease, peace, flow, loving kindness—the possibility of experiencing our true nature, which is Love. And then we might hear our inner wisdom, hear answers we've been seeking, be aware of the guidance being offered. But we can't fill a vessel that is already full. We need to let go and make space.

Part of letting go for me as 2018 began was using my guiding words for the new year: Love and Light and Yes! When I say I am Love and Light and I say Yes! to whatever is for my highest good, to aligning with my Higher Self, I move in trust, and then I can let go, be present, rest in the unknowing.

And yes, it's a daily practice. It sounds simple but I know it's not easy. It takes practice every day. I teach these concepts to better master them. It's all worth it in those moments when the light pours in and I feel the love. I say Yes! to receiving and being the Light and Love. I fill up with it and send it out to the world.

What is Reiki?

I love teaching Reiki. Maybe because it's all about love. Yes, we learn to do Reiki treatments in Reiki I and how to do long distance or remote treatments in Reiki II; and Reiki Masters may attune others to Reiki and teach Reiki. But in order to do all that, we need to be willing to open ourselves to the inherent Love that we already are.

Reiki is not an exclusive, separate energy that we are using to heal someone else. Reiki is simply the practice—the lifelong practice if you choose—of continually receiving or "channeling" the love that infuses us always, first for our healing. You can think of it from the Universe, God, Source, Spirit, All That Is, Nature, Inherent Good . . . everything, including us, are all the same loving energy. Reiki simply means Universal Life Force Energy.

Another wonderful thing about Reiki is how easily we can use it to treat ourselves. A self-treatment with Reiki can be just one minute, but just like meditating for one minute, that loving attention which makes space to return to our center can be profound and profoundly healing. For me, Reiki is always about connecting to our Higher Self where all our love resides. So, it's essentially a practice about Love. If we ever want to offer loving energy to others for them to use in their healing, we must give from a full vessel. So, the way I teach and practice Reiki is about filling up with this loving energy and letting it spill over in offering to all those around us, whether we do a hands-on treatment or not. The ceremony of the Reiki Attunement, which takes place in each class, helps open our channel, our receiving ability to the continuous flow of Universal Loving Energy of which we are an indivisible part. We consciously recognize this energy that is always available, but to which we do not always say YES!

Reiki helps us say YES! Yes to love. Yes to life. Yes to receiving and circulating that love to ourselves first. It has to start with us. The love we learn to flow in Reiki lubricates the gears of life, and that helps us have a smoother and more harmonious life experience.

And love is the greatest adventure there is.

Restoring, Regenerating, Healing

I talk a lot about taking loving care of ourselves, and that doing so is infinite and limitless. Nothing is once and done. We think we are taking loving care of ourselves, and we are, then life moves through us and we realize how we can take even more loving care of ourselves. We learn in baby steps. We don't get it all at once. That's what life is for, to learn about Love in steps that we can handle.

After being diagnosed with cancer in 2013, I took loving care of myself in a number of ways. And in the years following, that care kept evolving. In 2017, I felt even more deeply what loving care meant, and took additional steps to support my healing. Everyone's steps are different. Life is individual, and connected, all at the same time. As I take better care of myself, I fill up with the Love that is the Universal Life Force Energy. This love restores, regenerates and heals. And then I can spill over, give back, and take care of others from a strong and full place.

During my recovery, I've become aware that I have spent much of my lifetime draining my energy, leaking my energy, and giving my energy and bits and pieces of myself away. I didn't know how to take loving care of myself. I didn't know I had to fill myself up first. It has been a lifelong practice and a long time coming to love taking loving care of myself. I am so grateful that this work of love that has become my practice and my calling has given me the tools to fill, restore, regenerate, and heal.

And this is why I teach all of this. As I teach it every day, I hear it over and over, and I remind myself every day that I Am Love, I Love and I Am Loved. This is true for every one of us. To my mind, there is no better or fulfilling practice than that of a loving life.

And Love heals.

Making Space

I love my home and my family, including our four-legged fur baby, Little Bear. I love my practice, my friends, my clients. Life is good. I am grateful for the abundance of peace I feel now, in contrast to what life used to feel like. But sometimes I just need a break, a change of pace, a change of scenery. I just need to make some space where I am my only responsibility.

I realize the scale of my responsibilities pales in comparison with that of many others, but we each are living our own lives on our own paths. Comparing ourselves to others is a guarantee of suffering. Our own path, just how it is, will teach us about love and joy.

When I need space, I often go to my place of restoration and space, the beach, and usually just for an overnight. I do just what I want: walk on the beach, sit on the sand and watch the waves, read the kind of spiritual writings that feed my soul, eat good food, stay up late, maybe watch a little TV. I stay off the phone (for the most part, except calls home) and think. I make space.

And because of the space, there is room for feelings to be felt and awareness to rise up. I know we take ourselves wherever we go, and I know we need to find a way to make space and feel peace and joy in the middle of everyday life. I know we can't wait for time away or a vacation to let ourselves feel what we're holding and process it so we can let it go.

Holding unprocessed energy from all that we feel and think and do weighs on our bodies. Held long enough, that unprocessed energy can show up as pain, anxiety, worry. When we are consistently depressing something, we feel depression. And we can't wait for that vacation, that long weekend, the gap between jobs, kids leaving for college. We need to give ourselves the daily teeny tiny mini-vacation of just a pause, just a breath, just a bit of space.

I may have the luxury of going away overnight. But really, what would be the most loving to me would be to sit or lie quietly for just a few minutes each day and breathe. And perhaps think of walking on the beach and hearing the waves.

My Fantastic Voyage

As a kid, I loved the book *Fantastic Voyage* by Isaac Asimov. Maybe you remember it or the movie: "Four men and a woman are reduced to a microscopic fraction of their original size, sent in a miniaturized atomic sub through a dying man's carotid artery to destroy a blood clot in his brain. If they fail, the entire world will be doomed."

I no longer recall why the world would be doomed if the mission weren't successful, but I remember the idea of being inside the body and the fantastic and terrifying voyage that it was. Somehow this was brought to mind during one of my post cancer check-ups at the Duke Sarcoma Clinic.

I had finished with my treatment sometime in the summer of 2013, and since that time, I had been going to Duke every few months. Every time I went, I'd have a chest X-ray to check for metastasis. I had a choice as to how to handle the inevitable stress that accompanied each visit. Sometimes I was calm, aware of my breath, knowing I was taken care of no matter what the results were. Sometimes I was more nervous, concerned about some new unexplained lump, or what the X-ray would show. I navigated some visits more gracefully than others.

Along the way, I experienced incredible kindness on the part of the imaging department and the Sarcoma Clinic staff. There was the time I was in such fear, I was having a meltdown, crying through the X-ray. An angel named Lorenzo was the tech doing my X-ray. I had one of those moments where I am seeing a person, and hearing words, but feeling the winds and energy of pure Grace. We never know when Grace, or Spirit, will reach through the veil and touch us in a way we cannot miss. And that day, Lorenzo (who is now a supervisor) did just that. He comforted me, guided me, reassured me; he exuded Love. And all was well.

So, during this particular visit, my doctor told me we could consider this my five-year mark, and I only needed to come back once a year, for the next five years. He cautioned me that they never say "cured," but the chances of recurrence become less with each passing year.

I hadn't really given any thought to this transition before this appointment. I knew the protocol, but I wasn't waiting for any magic line of demarcation. So, I was unprepared for the rush of energy released, the emotion, the gratitude . . . the I'm not sure what . . . that I felt when he said five years, come back in a year, unless something comes up. I truly had no idea how much energy I was holding around the appointments, the scans, the X-rays, the uncertainty, the need to trust and let go. So, when those floodgates opened and the feelings poured through, I was surprised, and in awe.

We can hold and tamp down so much, reacting and responding to this fantastic voyage we call life. And then, at the right time, something lifts the lid on what we have been holding and managing and all that energy, or a layer of that energy, is released. On the heels of that release, so many seemingly forgotten memories surfaced that night. Once something got opened up, there was a pathway made for other energy that was ready to show itself to follow and be lovingly released.

The years since the cancer treatments have had a great many blessings in disguise. It's been quite a humbling journey, teaching me all the ways I need to take loving care of myself. As with everything else, my fantastic voyage is all about Love.

Riding the Wave

Everything in the Universe is moving energy, including us. And this energy is always moving around and through us in our day to day lives, expanding toward more good no matter what it may seem like. Sometimes we feel we are working in alignment with the natural flow of energy and sometimes we feel at cross purposes with this flow.

We perceive this energy in different ways. Life can feel very intense, or easier and more fluid. And our experience can change rapidly! I sometimes feel this energy as a huge wave pouring into the earth and us, and it is powerfully carrying us forward, ready or not. I've described it as hard and fast. The effect is that whatever we need to release, surrender or let go of is being cleared out of our mentality quickly and unceremoniously. It's like our Higher Self is saying: "You're done with this, this and that. Time to let go, NOW! It's in the way of where you are ready to go."

Where we are ready to go is always experiencing more love, which is our true nature, and seeing the manifestation of that in our lives through more health, wealth and happiness.

We are all on this journey together, as we are all interconnected, and love and trust is what eases our way and allows us to surf the wave rather than be dragged underneath along the sand and shells. One way or another, we are moving forward for our highest good. And we get to choose between the hard way or the easier, more supported way.

We have the support of all the Universe in our journey. We just have to ask and be willing to receive the response of the All, which will always come and will always be for our highest good, even if it doesn't look quite like what we expected!

I wish you the ride of your life.

Survive, Thrive and Flourish

A lot of my life has felt like an obstacle course I was just trying to survive. Through my metaphysical and spiritual studies, I was introduced to the idea that life was a wonderful, grand adventure. That made me scoff at first. I was just trying to get through, much less enjoy this so-called adventure.

But over time, as I kept laying in gossamer wings of willingness and good feeling (sometimes out of sheer desperation), I eventually reached the 51 percent threshold of being in joy, and then I began to shift from surviving to thriving—and finally flourishing. I make an effort to keep my wellspring of good feeling, my reservoir, filled beyond the 51 percent. Then if I tank because of some off-putting run-of-the-mill life experience (you know, the ones that happen every day), it's not such a stretch to forgive myself when I transgress and come back across the line. (Anyone else thinking "one toke over the line" right now?)

Flourishing has a life of its own. We have to work harder when we are at a deficit under 51 percent, because it takes energy to build energy. So, when we are below the 51 percent, it's a slower generating process. When we reach 51 percent, the energy exponentially builds on its own.

It's like our energy is joyously feeling our joy and we more effortlessly feel better and better. Or as it is said, the better it gets, the better it gets. Then joy becomes our touchstone instead of our longing.

Wishing you more joy than you can imagine in this grand adventure we call Life.

A Thousand Deaths

All relationships teach us something about Love. Our most difficult and/or longest lasting relationships are our Master Teachers. So long-term relationships of any kind offer innumerable opportunities for growth and learning—learning about loving ourselves, about staying on our own path and about staying in the present, which lends itself to feeling more joy.

It's tough to stay present when life feels as if it's moving at an accelerated pace. Here we are in this rocket we call Life, sometimes hanging on for dear life, or dear present-ness, much less taking in lessons about love and joy. The more I inhabit the present moment, the easier it is for me to stay grounded. The more grounded I feel, the more fully I am on my own path, the more I am able to tap into the support of all of the powerful loving energy of which we are an indivisible part. The more I am aware and allow the support of the waves of love and energy all around us, the less buffeted I feel.

So how do we sink into being present? We can always breathe, check in with the present moment, ask one of my favorite questions: what is happening right now? Is everything OK in this one moment? Yes, there are things to deal with and think about. But right now, in this slice of Now, if I really notice, if I am really willing, all is well, everything is OK. I am not flying off the edge of the Universe. I am completely taken care of. And then I check in with the next moment and the next. This is the gift and beauty of being willing to be present. This practice creates a spaciousness, a softening to the racing of life around us. It allows us to feel joy, in that exquisite, present moment, no matter what is happening. It allows us to sink into our true nature of peace and love.

When I am not present, I worry, I get anxious and overwhelmed. I'm thinking lots of what-ifs, telling myself stories that aren't true, creating scenarios with my imaginings that don't feel good. One particular incident really brought home this whole idea of being in the present moment, staying on my path, and how relationships are Master Teachers.

My husband is 26 years older than I am. In the past, I would often ask him, apropos of nothing in particular: Are you feeling OK? Are you all right? How are you doing? Of course, I was reading something dire into everything, worrying about his health, his age, worrying about him dying. (Not that there's any guarantee in life about who dies first.) After months of this he looked at me and said: "One day, I will die my one death. Don't have me die a thousand deaths before my one death!"

I got the message. It kicked me squarely back to the present, back onto my own path, and the possibility for inhabiting—and enjoying—this moment. Just as it is.

I invite you to take a breath and just feel what is truly happening in this moment, just this present moment.

The Queen of Re-frame

I have a friend who calls me the queen of re-frame. Re-frame as in: well, it may look like this but we can think of it like this! I actually prefer to think of it as looking at what is really true, instead of buying the story I might be telling myself or the story someone else might be telling.

For instance, I thought I wanted to have children. I couldn't have children, and now it has turned out that it was really for my highest good not to have kids. I've gotten to mother a lot of other people instead of my own kids and I relish the luxury of a simpler life without children. Certainly, my life is more suited to who I am and how I want to live, just as it is. And it makes time spent with my nephews and my friend's baby all the sweeter.

I was weeding our extremely overgrown garden one morning (to the delight and relief of our neighbors, I am sure). I could have been (and was) overwhelmed by how out of hand the weeds had gotten. Or I could have said, I love this abundance of growth! I welcome the abundance this symbolizes. Look how rich my life is! This joyous profusion of nature can hardly be contained!

While it may sound like re-framing is making lemonade out of lemons, I think it may be what is actually true, if we choose to look at a situation from a softer, more open, more trusting heart. Often, I am not aware of what is for my highest good, but in willingness and with surrender to my Higher Self, my true wisdom, it occurs anyway.

Some of the worst things in my life have been my greatest teachers, my greatest heart openers. They may have seemed disastrous at the time, but they were essential steps to who I am today. And everything in my life has contributed in some strange way to me loving and appreciating who I am now.

So maybe the greatest re-frame is to give up the idea that mistakes were made, and you'll never recover from or forgive yourself for some of the things done or said. We are always doing science experiments. If we didn't do something "wrong" or something that felt bad, or that we regretted, we'd never know what that felt like, and that enables us to make a different, more loving choice. By choosing to bless what doesn't work instead of condemning it, we have compassion for our flawed human selves and can be grateful for the opportunity to make a choice based in love.

And then we arrive at the ultimate re-frame: It's all good, and it's all about Love.

Grounding and Attaching
Our Silver Cord

When we are grounded, we are more able to be present. When we are present, it is easier to connect with our Higher Self, which is the Love that we are. When we connect with our Higher Self, it is easier to feel the peace and harmony that is inherently our true nature.

Grounding is essential to our spiritual health, and often to our physical health. We can't be "in our head" all the time. We need a balance. Even if the world is a difficult place to be in, we need to find a way to embrace our worldly body and life, while remembering we are truly Divine.

While we don't always feel it when we do grounding exercises, it's still important to practice grounding whether we feel it or not. I can attest to this. I grounded for years and couldn't feel it as I was doing the exercise, but I know it kept me more balanced and focused. My tendency is to live in the astral, to kind of always be "out there," and grounding brought me back to earth where I live and needed to be.

When we ground our energy, we connect with the cosmos and the earth, anchoring between them. Our Higher Self and the Universe are the perfect balance of yin and yang. Here on earth in our human condition, we vacillate in the balance of yin and yang, affected by all that is happening around us and within us. Grounding helps us balance and handle the influx of any change, within or without.

A simple grounding technique is to imagine the energies above you in the heavens. This is yang energy. Breathe in this swirl of energy through the top of your head. With continued gentle inhales and exhales, breathe it all the way through your body down to your feet, and then exhale the energy down into the heart of the earth. Now again with gentle inhales and exhales, breathe in the earth energy, the yin energy, all the way up through your body. The cosmic and earth energy will mix in just the right proportion in your body. You can send it with your intention just to where you need it most in your body. Just a few seconds several times during the day can stabilize and harmonize us.

Another way to ground ourselves is to attach our silver cord into our second chakra, our hara, and then send it all the way down to the center of the earth. I do this every night and during the day. It helps me with all the high frequency energy I use that can literally knock me off my feet sometimes.

Our hara is where our Higher Self energy sits in the body. *Hara* means ocean of energy. So, when we imagine inserting a silver cord (or whatever color you like) into our hara, about two inches below our naval, and then sending it down into the earth, we are grounding our Divine energy with the earth, intending balance. I do this at night because at night, we might travel out of our bodies processing energy, perhaps astral travel to ask for assistance and seek answers.

This might be what happens when we have those dreams that seem so real, or we suddenly understand something, or receive information that guides us.

When we attach the silver cord, we can see it extending above us, and we simply state that if we leave our body, we find our way back easily via our silver cord and our energies are seated firmly in our body before we wake. Sometimes I wake up feeling somewhat discombobulated and it takes me hours to feel settled in my body, and I realize I forgot to put in my silver cord. It makes a difference!

We move more effortlessly in our body when we are grounded. I know when I am ungrounded, I knock into things, drop things, fall over my feet. I used to think (and was told) I was clumsy. Now I realize I was just ungrounded.

Mother Earth is more than happy to offer up her nurturing, nourishing, loving, grounding energy. We have only to dip into her infinite wellspring and inhale the nectar.

A Humbling

I usually feel strong. Until I don't.

I recall a humbling couple of weeks when I wasn't strong at all. I have an inner ear condition that causes vertigo. It can be years between episodes, and well, you know, out of sight, out of mind. I'm aware of the triggers and I thought I was taking loving care of myself, until it became evident that I needed to be taking even better care of myself.

This is the beauty of having a physical body. We can feel what is happening, we often get the signals that leave no doubt. There are usually clues. Sometimes the evidence seems to blindside us, but when I look back at these times, the indications were there. I just can be very dense and resistant (like the rest of humanity) and ignore what is being broadcast loud and clear—in hindsight. And always, it boils down to needing to take better care of myself somehow, some way. More than I can imagine.

And then I use all my tools, usually out of desperation. Breathing, surrendering, being willing to know I don't know, resting, asking for and receiving assistance and guidance, being willing to meet my distress with grace and trust. Trust that everything changes, everything passes. Eventually.

So, yet another humbling experience. Remembering that we never know what we don't know until we do. Remembering that we are all taken care of, that life lives through us, life doesn't persecute us. Remembering what it feels like to be ill, unable to work, debilitated. In my gratitude for feeling better, I have more compassion for those who don't feel better—ever. Could I meet a condition that never lifted with grace and trust? Would I know I was always taken care of, no matter what?

Through various illnesses and challenges, the proof is always presented that we get through everything. Life continues to move on; it is never static. Situations eventually change. The energy always moves. Would that the next time, in the middle of whatever arises, I have more equanimity, more trust, and more grace than I can imagine. I wish you the same.

Take Good Loving Care of Yourself

I often say to my clients and students: Take good loving care of yourself!

To which a woman once responded, "When you say to 'take good loving care' of myself, I picture eating my vegetables or getting some exercise . . . maybe more hot baths. Is that what you mean?"

I told her it could be.

When you take good loving care of yourself, not only is it "good for you," but there is joy in doing it. If eating your vegetables isn't joyous and doesn't taste good, but you feel you "should" eat them, that's not very loving. If getting some exercise feels good, circulates your good feeling, then that's loving! If you love hot baths, great. If you don't, taking them is not going to feel good or circulate good feeling.

And what constitutes taking good loving care of yourself can change over time. At 63 years, I had never done weight lifting or barbell workouts. But when a new gym opened nearby, I started working out there, but only because I was being prompted by my inner voice (to my surprise). And I knew it was good for my body for bone strength. I thought, well, maybe this could be loving. What surprised me is how I felt about it. I used to say I love walking and yoga and that's it—and not walking in the heat. I can be limiting, restrictive, picky . . . one might even say (and some have) high maintenance.

What I discovered by being willing to try something new is that I love finding I can do something I never thought I could do—or would want to do. The training almost immediately made a difference in my strength and my body. I felt more confident in my body and how it moved. And it helped my yoga practice, too.

I have a friend in his 70s who has been studying Spanish for a number of years. It is one of the most loving things he can do for himself. He is challenged, it's sociable, and he has learned so much about people from other cultures. As he can speak to others, he gets to know them and their humanity. Very loving.

Sometimes it takes a while before we can hear the message about what is most loving for us. Or we judge the message we hear. Sometimes it's lounging on the couch and watching TV. Sometimes it's sleeping in. Sometimes it's having a whole can of whipped cream. And sometimes it's eating vegetables we love.

Sometimes it means going to the doctor, or taking medications, or having surgery or radiation. Sometimes it's cutting back on meds, or choosing not to have treatment or surgery. For me, it can mean calling my sister when I am in the throes of despair. Other times it's seeing my nephews or hanging out at home with my family and kitty. Sometimes it's shopping therapy! Sometimes it's holding classes, and sometimes it's not holding a class. And sometimes it's being quiet and alone. It's all completely individual.

It takes willingness to ask: What is the most loving thing I can do for myself today, or right now, in this moment? I ask all the time. I don't always want to hear the answer. I don't always want to do what is the most loving thing for me. My human side can be very resistant. I don't want to cancel that appointment! I want to show up! I don't want to go through that paperwork! I don't want to do the bookkeeping or make that phone call. But if I continue to ignore what my loving Higher Self is telling me, or what the people who love me lovingly suggest, I suffer.

So, with willingness and curiosity, we hear the answers more clearly. With practice, we learn to take better loving care of ourselves. It's baby steps. And it's being the Love we truly are. And we have a whole lifetime to practice.

Unconditional Love

Who or what or how are we loving when we practice unconditional love? Are we loving terrorists? Are we loving people who have terrorized us in our lives? Murderers? Rapists? Well, we don't love the human selves or behavior that perpetrate such atrocities. But we do love the Higher Self of each individual, the loving energy that they are, that we all are, but from which they are disconnected.

In spiritual work, we are often instructed or encouraged to love everyone. Seldom are we told about loving ourselves as well as everyone else. If we can't see our light and love, it's difficult to see the light of others.

The Buddha says, "You yourself, as much as anybody in the entire universe, deserve your love and affection."

According to physician and author Christiane Northrup, "No matter what you're feeling, the only way to get a difficult feeling to go away is simply to love yourself for it. If you think you're stupid, then love yourself for feeling that way. It's a paradox, but it works. To heal, you must be the first one to shine the light of compassion on any areas within you that you feel are unacceptable."

We are all a part of the same light, the same radiance. It is a very difficult practice to love ourselves, let alone others. If we are judgmental of our frailties and flaws, we most certainly will be judging others. As we develop compassion for our self, we can extend that compassion to others, as we all plod through this challenging human life. The loving kindness and compassion we flow to ourselves fills us up and spills over to others . . . and we can't flow from an empty well.

I have a practice I use to help myself and others see the light in ourselves and others. This is a practice; it once took me three years to learn to love the Higher Self of someone who had betrayed and hurt me deeply. It's a pretty simple practice, but I had to practice every day. Here's how you do it.

Think of someone in your life who loves you unconditionally and you love them unconditionally (this could even be your kitty or dog or other four-legged loving being—sometimes it's easier with them). Now imagine their spirit beyond their visible or physical or human form. Imagine the pure light that makes up this loving being. Now imagine the light of the Universe behind this loving being. Next, see yourself as a part of this picture—all of the light of the Universe giving light to the being you are thinking of and that same light infusing you. Now we are seeing the Higher Self, or true nature of our self and the one we love. This is the easy part.

Now ask to see the light of the person you are having trouble loving. Not their human self—their radiant, loving, light-filled Spirit, their Higher Self. THIS is what we love. This may be difficult. Usually we see the human self that is so unloving. So be willing to set their human self aside, and focus on their light. All of us, everything, comes from this loving, radiant energy. Even if a human is despicable, they still have this light, their Higher Self. They are just not making any effort to be the light, to allow that light to flow through them, or they are denying it altogether. They make a choice for the least amount of love.

When I do this practice, I often see the human of the person I'm working with as sitting in a parched, desolate desert with no water or nourishment. When we disconnect from the Love we are, from our Higher Self, we are in dire straits. We are in pain. We are shut off from what feeds and supports us. But the balm and regeneration of the Love we are is always available. We just may be so captured by our ego that we have completely forgotten there is more to us than our human form.

So, we don't love bad behavior. We don't forgive all the terrible things that have been inflicted on us. But our true work is circulating love and good feeling, to ourselves first. So ultimately, we forgive ourselves for holding back our loving feeling. And then we love the Spirit, the Light, the Higher Self of the person who has wronged us, and feel the succor and peace that comes from being willing to flow and be the Love that we are. And we can ask the person—silently—to open their heart to the love being offered. And they will or they won't. It's their choice and not our business.

When I do this practice, I also see the Higher Self of the unloving person as reaching out to them with open arms, always available for loving connection, to remind them of who they truly are. We can't truly be disconnected from our Spirit, our Higher Self, but through our free will choice to turn away from the Love we are, we are capable of acting in monstrous ways.

When we do this practice with an open and willing heart, it is amazing how we can eventually flow love to everyone and everything. I send clouds of loving light to everyone on the planet and beyond every day. And all the people in the world who sometimes make me crazy are wonderful opportunities for practicing love—daily!

You are Love. Be the Love you are. Just Love. Your beloved self, first.

Being of Service

I often ruminate about being of service and I sometimes have trouble with this subject. This is because when some spiritual disciplines and religions speak about service, it is spoken of in a way as to indicate that loving the self, taking loving care of ourselves, is selfish. That to be spiritual we must be self-sacrificial. That altruism forgets the kindly, loving care of self and thinks only of others. It seems the goal is to forget the self in service of others.

I have a different awareness of service. I first must be in service to myself by expressing myself authentically in the most true and loving way for me. This is always our responsibility and no one else's. No one else can know our path or what is right for us. No one else knows if our heart is singing, or what makes it sing!

As we flow our good feeling, doing what feels good, which can be a simple thing such as sitting on the swing on the back deck, or doing the work we love, or the work with which we are presented at the moment, we fill up our reservoir. NOW we have a full or fuller vessel from which to give. Now we aren't scraping the bottom of the barrel.

As I am just being me, teaching what I love in the way I love and understand, I am being of service in the way I have been called on to be in my life. And it uplifts and fills me! As I do what I love, I am joyous that others feel that love and receive it! And it flows back to me, and I receive it, and have more to give, in an endless cycle (until, being human, we temporarily lose our way and halt the cycle . . . until we recover). And every step along the way, every wacky step, every step where I seemed to lose my way, was essential and perfect, just as each step unfolded, to bring me to this moment of fullness and joy and service. I had to be in service to myself first, be willing to find what makes my heart sing, what feels loving to me, what reminds me of the Love I am, which fills me up so I can spill over to others.

Richard Rohr, who I think of as a radically loving Franciscan, talked about this in his meditation "Who Am I?" He quotes Dr. Howard Thurman (1899-1981), theologian and civil rights leader.

Dr. Thurman says: "Don't ask what the world needs. Ask what makes you come alive, and go do it. Because what the world needs is people who have come alive."

Rohr writes: "As conscious human beings, our life purpose is to be a visible expression of both the image and the likeness of God. Each of us reveals a unique facet of the divine, what Franciscan John Duns Scotus called *haecceity* or *thisness*."

American author, educator and activist Parker Palmer says it well in his book *Let Your Life Speak*:

"[My newborn granddaughter] did not show up as raw material to be shaped into whatever image the world might want her to take. She arrived with her own gifted form, with the shape of her own sacred soul . . . . Thomas Merton calls it true self. Quakers call it the inner light, or "that of God" in every person. The humanist tradition calls it identity and integrity. No matter what you call it, it is a pearl of great price . . . .

"The deepest vocational question is not, "What ought I to do with my life?" It is the more elemental and demanding, "Who am I? What is my nature?" . . . [I believe we've got to get our own who right before we can begin to address the question of what am I to do.]

"Our deepest calling is to grow into our own authentic selfhood, whether or not it conforms to some image of who we ought to be. As we do so, we will not only find the joy that every human being seeks—we will also find our path of authentic service in the world. True vocation joins self and service, as Frederick Buechner (in *Wishful Thinking: A Seeker's ABC*) asserts when he defines vocation as "the place where your deep gladness meets the world's deep need" . . . .

"Contrary to the conventions of our thinly moralistic culture, this emphasis on gladness and selfhood is not selfish. The Quaker teacher Douglas Steere was fond of saying that the ancient human question "Who am I?" leads inevitably to the equally important question "Whose am I"—for there is no selfhood outside of relationship . . . .

"The world still waits for the truth that will set us free—my truth, your truth, our truth—the truth that was seeded in the earth when each of us arrived here formed in the image of God. Cultivating that truth, I believe, is the authentic vocation of every human being."

And one of my favorite pieces on this subject is a letter to Agnes De Mille from Martha Graham, both iconic American dancers. Here is part of it:

"There is a vitality, a life force, a quickening that is translated through you into action, and because there is only one of you in all time, this expression is unique. And if you block it, it will never exist through any other medium and be lost. The world will not have it. It is not your business to determine how good it is nor how valuable it is nor how it compares with other expressions. It is your business to keep it yours clearly and directly to keep the channel open. You do not even have to believe in yourself or your work. You have to keep open and aware directly to the urges that motivate YOU."

It's all about love, and loving you, first, so you can then love and be of service to others.

The Fog of Depression

Fog

*The fog comes
on little cat feet.*

*It sits looking
over harbor and city
on silent haunches
and then moves on.*

— Carl Sandburg

Engaging in our spiritual work gives us a sense of comfort and security. We think that if we align with our higher selves and think about being the Love that we are and want to see in the world, then we will avoid the pain and suffering in life. If I make every effort to act in accordance with the Love I am, life will be smooth sailing. Well, sometimes that's true, but then life happens.

And no matter what we do, sometimes the fog of depression comes in. If you haven't felt that fog approaching and then enveloping you, it's hard to explain. If you have felt it, you know what I'm talking about. It doesn't always arrive on little cat feet; sometimes it swipes at us and we are blindsided. And while it does eventually move on, we never know when that will be.

We often don't know what brings on depression. Sometimes we are depressed because we are depressing something that we are feeling or something we need to hear. Sometimes we are depressing a question to which we don't want to hear the answer. Or we are attached to the answer being a certain something . . . and now we are suffering. Or we are fearful, or anxious or worried, and we're not sure why. We may even be willing to be curious and open up our energy and say, I need help, I receive it, I am willing to hear the answer no matter what it is. But still we feel that fog and have no idea why. We don't always need to know why, or we may never know why. And that's OK, too.

We may try everything: exercise, breathing, meditation, healthy food, praying, focusing on connecting with our higher selves, taking loving care of ourselves in every way possible, talking with those we love. However, these are not vaccines to keep us immune from fear, anxiety, depression, worry. The panacea is often a holistic approach, a combination of many things. We need to be willing to do everything necessary, including acknowledging and honoring that we are in human form, in a body. And sometimes the body needs medicine, as the mind might need therapy, or meditation.

Just like one thing alone doesn't usually cause our depression or disease or whatever we're dealing with, there is often a plethora of remedies we need to employ. The cumulative effect of life's experiences and stresses can bring something on over time, and we often need a tapestry of solutions. We heal, bit by bit.

When I was younger, the waves of depression would slam into me without warning and might take months to lift. Now I am more aware of these signs and signals that often feel like the auras that can occur before a migraine. This disruption to my energy flow is always a call to be kinder and more compassionate to myself. And the sooner I respond, the more quickly and easily the heavy energy moves.

The little cat feet pad away. And once I again, I feel my true, loving self. She was there all along.

Wholeness

In the infinity of life where I am, all is perfect, whole, and complete.

— Louise Hay

The idea of a fractured, broken self is untrue in reality, although it feels very real when we're experiencing it. We think of reality as what our human self is going through. But our human reality is fleeting and temporary. So, everything here feels real—all the joy, all the pain, all the success, all the suffering. But it truly is temporary. Our human lives are only for a time. Our Spirit, the energy we are that animates our human body, is what is real, permanent, immortal, part of the Divine—the part of us that never dies. It transforms. This is the infinity of life that Louise Hay is speaking of.

I find it useful to use the words temporary and unreal interchangeably. Human life is temporary (unreal) in the sense that it eventually ends. Our Spirit is permanent and real (Spirit doesn't end and neither does our spirit, our energy). There is a phrase in metaphysics: Only the good is real. I finally understood and resolved this by understanding that the good is Spirit (God, Love) and that is permanent and that is what is real. While our human condition feels real, it is unreal in that it is temporary and will pass. Remembering our true loving nature can help us respond more compassionately to our human challenges and circumstances, and infuse whatever life we are having with more ease, light and joy.

It has often been said that we are spiritual beings having a temporary human experience. The truth of our true being, our inherent nature of Love, is that we are every moment whole, perfect and complete. Our human experience feels so very real, and while we are here, we must deal with our experiences and our pain. We pay attention to what hurts first and always with extreme kindness and compassion to ourselves. In this way, we begin to heal the rift we think has occurred between our human and Divine selves. We often feel so separate from our loving being, but in actuality, that rift can never occur between our human self and our authentic, true spiritual eternal being. We just may temporarily be unable to feel "the rest of us" when we are so focused on our human experience and condition. We can never actually be separate from our Higher Self, from Spirit, from the Love that we are. We are always indivisibly a part of All That Is, Spirit, Love. We just don't always remember it, or feel it. And that's OK. It goes along with being human. And we just keep coming back to who we really are as soon as we can. Willingness, kindness, love and compassion are the keys.

No matter how human we feel and no matter how much we feel all that goes along with being human, this lifetime provides us the opportunity to heal the separation between our human self and our

Divine self. As we remember our true nature and feel it (often in baby steps), we feel and remember the truth of our wholeness. And as we feel our true being, our Higher Self, then we begin to feel and remember the Love we are. And since our true being is part of the whole Oneness which is all love, when we remember our wholeness, we also remember the strength and power of that love. Therein truly lies our healing . . . connecting with the power that comes from the sense of wholeness and the feeling and awareness that we are love. And since love is the most powerful force in the Universe, when we are anchored in the Love we are, we are less likely to be knocked off our center, no matter what happens.

This is why Lao Tzu (an ancient Chinese philosopher and writer who is the reputed author of the *Tao Te Ching* and the founder of philosophical Taoism) said:

Practice love until we remember we are love.

Anger

*Of the Seven Deadly Sins, anger is possibly the most fun.
To lick your wounds, to smack your lips over grievances
long past, to roll over your tongue the prospect of bitter
confrontations still to come, to savor to the last toothsome
morsel both the pain you are given and the pain you are
giving back—in many ways it is a feast fit for a king.
The chief drawback is that what you are wolfing down is
yourself. The skeleton at the feast is you.*

— Frederick Buechner

Anger often comes up when we are in Mercury retrograde, that time
when everything gets re-evaluated and re-assessed. Old issues and
patterns return for review and re-experiencing and reflection . . . and
releasing. We get to see all of our resistance all over again. Think
of everything beginning with "re" and you get the idea of Mercury
retrograde.

The *Old Farmer's Almanac* says: "Due to the way our own orbit
interacts with those of the other planets, they might sometimes appear

to be traveling backward through the night sky with respect to the zodiac. This is, in fact, an illusion, which we call apparent retrograde motion.

"Several times a year, it appears as if Mercury is going backwards. These times in particular were traditionally associated with confusion, delay, and frustration.

"Perhaps Mercury's retrograde periods can cause our plans to go awry. However, this is an excellent time to reflect on the past. It's said that intuition is high during these periods, and coincidences can be extraordinary."

The Roman god Mercury is commonly identified with the Greek Hermes, the fleet-footed messenger of the gods. Thus, Mercury retrograde is associated with problems with messages, such as communications, electronic glitches, misunderstandings. I've noticed phone issues where the signals don't flow or connect smoothly.

And while I generally feel more flowing and smoother day to day at this point in my life, old ways of thinking or reacting definitely flare up at times. Old pools of unresolved energy are unexpectedly triggered, and I overreact to the present-day situation. And anger is an old way of reacting. I notice the agitation to something minor or the short answer or the sharp tone, all of which hurt me more than the person to whom they are directed.

The more we practice Love, the more we notice when we depart from Love. We have less slack! And this is a good thing. When we notice how anger cuts off our good feeling like a vise, and forgive ourselves and return to our loving being as soon as we can, then we are not giving in to the anger, but rather letting it serve us.

I remember a student in one of my metaphysics classes once saying: "But it feels good to be angry!" Sometimes we just need to be angry . . . until it doesn't entertain us or feel good anymore. We'll get there at the right time and let go of it, forgive ourselves and return to our true loving nature.

Frederick Buechner speaks of anger chillingly. But truly, even dealing with anger is all about Love. Remember and practice the Love you are, and don't be the skeleton at the feast.

Emptying

Every word, thought and action is energy. We are constantly processing these bits of energy so as to keep moving forward in a smooth fashion through our lives. But because so much happens in daily life, it's not possible to process all of that energy, clear it out and start with a clean slate every day.

Our true mission, our true work in life beyond what we do for a living, is to circulate love and good feeling, to ourselves first. There are many ways of taking loving care of ourselves. One of my ways is to periodically retreat to the beach. Standing on the ocean's edge, I give everything up I have been holding on to that is cluttering up my energy field. I have other ways of clearing my energy field and processing collected remnants of energy: every night when I get into bed, I do my Medical Qi Gong breathing, my self-Reiki, and I state my intention to release everything I may have collected during this day and before, and am now ready to surrender. Doing kidney breaths all during the day helps me empty bits and pieces of energy I may have taken on during the course of the day.

And always, quiet times and meditation (however brief) contribute to my well-being and smooth flow. But my favorite spot is at the edge of the ocean. This is where my heart sings.

I grew up on the Pacific Ocean beaches of Southern California. It was a good symbol for the first part of my life: wilder, unpredictable and less settled. The Atlantic Ocean, while it can be fierce in times of storm and hurricane, has a softness and warmth, particularly in the summer, that the Pacific Ocean never has. Yes, the Atlantic can be treacherous with its rip currents, just like the cliffs and cold and rogue waves of the Pacific in Northern California can be. But at the same time both are magnificent and breathtaking and require respect and care, just like our beloved selves.

Sometimes as I release and become clearer and lighter, I feel completely empty and open to the present moment. And then my human mind crops up and says wait, what would happen if we were completely empty? What would happen to me, the me that I think is the true me? But that me is not my true self, the I Am . . . and then I catch the ego in one of its tricks and release again.

The true self is Love. The true self, the I Am, is not the I/me/ego of the human self that is our necessary partner in this life. That me is the ego that dies with the body. The true self is what lives on, our energy that transforms into that love and light. As a favorite person of mine says, there is no I in love. All the love flows from our Higher Self and infuses our human experience as much as we are able and willing to allow and receive it. The I/me/ego is only as loving as our alignment with our Higher Self.

It's an ongoing journey to take loving care of ourselves. Emptying, releasing, surrendering, letting go into the good or God is one way of taking loving care of ourselves. Sometimes that journey includes a trip to the ocean. The vast water and endless waves and innate wisdom can take all our detritus in and transform it into light and love.

When I stand with my feet in the water, or on the beach with the wind blowing through me, I have an opportunity to empty all the flotsam and jetsam that has stuck to my energy field. As I release, give up, surrender, I remember I am that clear glass of water that began this lifetime. For a while I remember that heaven is right here on earth.

Metaphysical Trinity

Everything flows from within, out. From invisible to visible. From Source, One Mind, Spirit, to physical form. Everything has to be completed in Spirit, in energy, in the invisible, before it can appear in our visible world. When we want to manifest something, bring something to fruition, there are actual mechanics, an actual system that we can use and rely upon to bring things from invisible to visible, from unseen to seen. And it works no matter what we are working with; it works in all directions. I call this system the Metaphysical Trinity.

Since this is a Trinity, there are three distinct steps:

Desire: What you want—your vision, idea, wish

Knowing: Thinking—doing your part, letting go, flowing love and good feeling

Feeling: 51 percent certainty, love and good feeling—making space to receive—giving birth to the manifestation

And remember, you can't always get what you want, but you just might get what you need, as some very wise contemporary—and rock 'n roll—philosophers once said. No matter what we ask for, we need to remember we don't always know what is for our highest good. So, at the end of our process, we also state:

This or something better, whatever is for my highest good. I'm willing to hear the answer no matter what it is. We embrace it all, whatever it is.

Desire

The first step is just what is says: What do you want? What is your desire, wish, vision? How do you want a situation different from what it is now? It's not useful to wish another person were different; but we can ask for help for our behavior that we want to change. When I'm not eating as well as I want, or moving my body as much as I like, if I'm having difficulty with a decision or situation in my life, I first ask for help and state my desire, before I do anything else.

Knowing

The second step is what comprises our part, our responsibility, the logistics, the actual details and things we need to do, what we need to think about and sort through. Often, this is where we see our resistance. We want chocolate ice cream, but we want it to magically appear in front of us without going to the ice cream shop, or ordering it online to have it delivered to us. We must do our part. The Universe, God, Source is indivisibly connected to us, joined at the hip, so to speak. When we ask, there is always a response of some kind. But we have to ask (first step, desire) which gives the Universe permission to help us. We have free will, nothing gets imposed on us, even assistance from the All. And then we do our part, fulfilling our responsibility in the matter.

If you want something that is not happening, you have to look at where are you blocking your love and good feeling. This is part of the second step. Think of love and good feeling as the lubrication of the gears that brings to you what you want—or what is for your highest good. Without the lubrication of the feeling of love nothing can be brought into manifestation. Love gives birth to everything good! So, part of our second step is to ask: Where am I holding back my good feeling?

Some years ago, I was feeling a lot of lack and not enough abundance. I had to ask myself: Where am I holding back good feeling? What ill feeling am I holding on to? And as soon as I asked, the answer was clear: I was still holding on to ill feeling about someone who had caused great harm and loss in my life, years after the event. Of course, I had responsibility too: I ignored many red flags, didn't listen to my Higher Self. So, to restore my good feeling (again, part of the second step), I forgave myself for thinking I could have done anything differently at the time (I was too fearful) and began the process of being willing to love this person's Higher Self, that is pure love, just like all of us. I didn't forgive the bad behavior; that person will have to do that for themselves. But I was willing to restore the flow of love and good feeling, first to me, and then sending love to the loving, pure spirit of the person I felt had wronged me. And I asked that person's human self to open their heart to the love being sent. Whether they did or didn't was their business, not mine. My responsibility was to send the love where it could be received, to their Higher Self, their soul, their spirit.

Then I recognized all the abundance I did have in my life right then. I looked around at my garden and my hundreds of abundantly blooming irises, and saw the picture of my abundance right at that very moment. The abundance of nature is always a good reminder of the abundance that naturally exists that we are always a part of. And in small steps, I built up layers of good feeling, and over time, got to 51 percent good feeling, and my abundance flowed in all ways. And I never looked back.

Now, when I start to feel tight, or restricted, or lacking, I immediately take responsibility for where I am shutting down or slowing my flow of good feeling—sometimes to a trickle. And even if I don't know, I simply say, whatever I am holding on to that is closing off my good feeling, I release, and make space for more good than I can imagine. If I can be made aware of what I am doing or thinking, great. I'm willing to take responsibility and do the process even if I'm not ready to hear what I'm holding onto.

If you are looking for a new job, new house, new relationship, resolution or anything else, you need to be willing (which flows our good feeling) to do whatever steps are necessary. We always need to be willing to do whatever is necessary. Look on websites, contact a realtor, go on interviews, network, consult people you trust, whatever feels good. People may say, well I really don't want to work. And I say: What is the most loving thing you can do for yourself? Do you want to pay your bills? Then the most loving thing is dropping your resistance to working and being willing to do whatever is necessary for your highest good. That doesn't mean taking a job you hate, because that will just close down your good feeling again. Even if we take a job that is not our first choice, we can choose to flow good feeling around it because it is serving us in some way.

The important thing to remember is that all of what we do, all of our efforts that are part of "our part" as opposed to the part of the Universe, is to move the energy. What shows up may not be a direct result of what we do. The job we get may not come from the resumes we send out, it may come to us some way we can't even imagine. We may sign up on a dating site, and even go out on dates, and the person we wind up loving may not come from that avenue at all. It isn't that if we do this, then that will happen. It's that we're willing to move the energy doing whatever is necessary, whatever we can do with an open and willing heart, and maintaining anticipatory eagerness for what will unfold. We are trusting we are part of All That Is Good.

When I talk about this, I illustrate the point by rubbing my hands together and saying, I can't wait to see what happens! Before all the amazing things that happened in our lives, we didn't know the moment before. Before you knew you passed the licensing exam, found your love, your job, your home, before a situation finally changed, we didn't know the moment before it happened. The answer, solution, resolution, can happen in an instant.

After we have done everything we can think of to further or resolve a situation, there is one more vital step: we have to let go. Once we have handled all the details and logistics, we let go. At this point, I open my hands palms up, and say out loud, I've done everything I know to do, I let it go for the Universe to take over and start pulling all the threads of the tapestry that I don't see. I don't see the whole picture. My Higher Self, Spirit, sees the forest while I just see the trees. Since we are all an indivisible part of the Whole, the Whole comes into play to resolve any situation. It's not just up to us, we are a co-creator with Spirit, with the energy of the Universe. But we must let go to make space for the answer to be dropped in. If we are continually fiddling with the issue, the Universe says, I've got an answer for you, but there's no space to drop it in, you're filling all the space! Let go, make some room, and you will see the solution. Everything must be completed in Spirit, in the invisible, before it migrates into the visible, into our experience. We have to let go, in trust and faith, for that to happen.

When something is not resolving, I will always ask the person if they have done everything necessary. Is there anything they're holding back that they or their inner voice knows or thinks they have to do? Invariably, people will say, oh yes, I've done everything! And still the situation doesn't resolve. And eventually, it turns out there was just a little something that someone felt couldn't be important enough. But it was that piece of resistance, of unwillingness, that slowed down the flow. They were not quite fulfilling their part. And as soon as that resistance was given up and the person did truly the everything necessary, the situation resolved. And sometimes only we know what we are holding onto, what is blocking the flow.

In one case, someone couldn't sell a wonderful house. The issue holding back their flow of good feeling was resisting repainting a room, or fixing the grout in the bathroom. It seemed good enough. But. . . they knew. And once they dropped the resistance and did truly the "everything necessary," the house immediately went under contract. They were almost at the 51 percent and just tipped over the threshold and the buyer showed up.

Feeling

And then we come to the third step, which is receiving the answer, the resolution. Remember the letting to? Letting go is a prelude to receiving. I hold my arms open in a big circle in front of me and say, I release this to the Universe, I make space to receive the answer, no matter what it is. And if there's anything else I need to do, give it back to me and I will take care of it, and release it again. And then we build our feeling to 51 percent certainty that it is already done, perfectly. We believe it, trust it, before we see it. We have to be 51 percent certain (and sometimes the answer comes, the solution is presented, and we didn't even realize we were at 51 percent). And then everything comes together and we see, in the visible, in our human world, the answer to our request.

The beauty of this system is that it puts you in touch with your power, and that power is the Love you are. Flowing that love helps you change how you respond to what is happening in your life. If you don't like what you are experiencing or how you are feeling, you get to think of something else that you would like and follow this process. We focus on what we want, not what we don't want. We don't deny what's happening; we need to be aware so we can make a different choice.

It doesn't matter what we are dealing with; this system works for everything in all directions. We just may not get the answer we want, and then we have to deal with our expectations and attachments.

We can bring ourselves to a feeling of 51 percent certainty about something erring or true. We prove how powerful both our ego and our love are. We have free will to choose for Love or not. Anything that is human or comes from ego is temporary, no matter how distressing or terrible it is. Evil may be temporary, but is horrifying in the human world. The good news is, everything human ends. Only that which comes from Love is real and permanent and true. And we are indivisibly connected to the Source from which all loving power flows.

If we experience something we don't like, we're not being punished for what we thought. We are experiencing the causative power of thought and feeling for our benefit. It shows us truly how powerful we are, being a part of the All! When we witness the results of our thinking to a feeling of conclusion we can decide if this is what we want. Sometimes we come to erring conclusions out of fear, ignorance or erring suppositions or beliefs. If we don't like what we see, we have the ability to marshal our response (taking response-ability, having the ability to respond) to what we are experiencing in life or witnessing in ourselves. We have free will to do a new science experiment. Sometimes it is hard to get a handle on the thoughts buzzing around in our head, and they seem to have a life of their own. But in truth, we are in charge of our thoughts. Not that it's easy . . . but our true nature of Love is the most powerful force in the universe, and with practice, the Metaphysical Trinity helps us flow the Love we are.

This process happens over and over again in life because this is Earth School, as Gary Zukav says in *Seat of the Soul*. We are in the classroom of Life.

We Can Hold Both

A friend of mine is moving across country. She is happy to move, and the house hunting is very challenging . . . and she is happy to move. Both are true. We can hold both. It's not black or white, one thing or another. It's both at the same time. And that's OK!

We humans like things to be very clear-cut; we often think in terms of black or white, either/or. We wish everything would go smoothly all the time. We don't like the ups and downs. But life happens and the way to navigate the rapids that will for sure come is to be aware that we have a choice in how we respond. It's not about stopping the waves. It's about learning to surf them more easily.

Shakespeare said: " . . . for there is nothing either good or bad, but thinking makes it so…nothing is really good or bad in itself—it's all what a person thinks about it." This explains why some people look at a situation and see it as terrible while others simply don't think it's a big deal. We see this in our society all the time.

What if we didn't need to take it one way or the other? That sometimes the people we love are wonderful, and sometimes they disappoint us? Relationships are not meant to be perfect all the time, or necessarily easy. We are meant to learn about Love in relationship. Loving is not a done deal once we're in a relationship. It's on ongoing process. And everyone on all sides of a relationship always has something to learn about Love.

One of my favorite quotes about Love is from Anne Morrow Lindbergh in her book *Gift From the Sea*: "When you love someone you do not love them all the time, in exactly the same way, from moment to moment. It is an impossibility. Security in a relationship lies neither in looking back to what it was in nostalgia, nor forward to what it might be in dread or anticipation, but living in the present relationship and accepting it as it is now."

Jack Kornfield has a wonderful writing on opening to being in the moment with everything just as it is, embracing all of it. Here's a piece of it from his essay "Stop the War Within."

"With mindfulness and compassion we can let go of our battles and open our heart with kindness to things just as they are. Then we come to rest in the present moment. This is the beginning and the end of spiritual practice. Only in the present moment can we discover that which is timeless. Only here can we find the love that we seek. Love in the past is a memory, and love in the future is fantasy. Only in the reality of the present can we love, can we awaken, can we find peace and understanding and connect with ourselves and the world."

Tibetan Buddhist Surya Das writes:

"The sublime peace of the Tao [is] something we can all experience by . . . coming into accord with how things actually are—what

Tibetan Buddhists call the natural state. Rather than trying to build skyscrapers to reach heaven and bridges to cross the raging river of samsara (wandering the cycles of life) to reach the so-called other shore of nirvana, we could realize that it all flows right through us right now and there's nowhere to go, nothing to get, and all is perfect as it is. This deep inner knowing has a lot to do with trust and letting be; there is nirvanic peace in things just as they are."

Holding some discomfort at the same time as holding some comfort is not easy. There is usually something going on that we like as well as something we don't. But if we can hold both, if we can hold all of it, embrace all of it just as it is, then our heart is softened and eased and our life is simplified. Then we can respond from and with Love—to all of it.

It's All About Love

How can it be all about Love in this crazy world of ours? It almost sounds like an oxymoron. It may sound over-simplistic, but it really is simple. It's just not easy. It takes a lot of practice. It's like the saying, think globally and act locally. We love right where we are, starting with ourselves, which can be very challenging. But when we love right where we are, who we are (locally), we then fill up with that love and spill it over to everyone and everything around us (globally).

I talk to many people about so many situations, so many different details. Whatever the variation, one of the first questions I ask is: What's the most loving thing you can do for yourself in this situation? If we do what is most loving, for our highest good and the highest good of all concerned, then we move in more love for us and everyone around us. This is how we fill up and spill over with love.

This may sound selfish. But self-care is very loving, not selfish. If we are not doing what is loving for us, then we become angry, resentful, bitter. We blame the other person. If we are seated in our power—and power means our love, as love is the most powerful force in the Universe—and are willing to ask, hear and act upon what is loving to us, we will be more loving to everyone around us. Not that everyone will be happy when we take loving care of ourselves. If someone is not getting what they want from us, or not taking loving care of themselves, they may not like that we are taking loving care of ourselves. But it is our responsibility to identify what makes our hearts sing, what is loving for us. No one else lives in our minds or hearts. No one else really knows what is loving for us. Only we know. We might tell someone else, share these ideas, but we have the primary responsibility for taking loving care of us. Yes, we can compromise, but we can't compromise or transgress our true selves. If we transgress what's true for us, we are not acting in our highest good or the highest good of all concerned.

It's also all about love in relationships, even if the relationship is not as loving as we would like. In a relationship, everyone experiences exactly what they are meant to experience. Each person is in the relationship to learn about love. It's all about love! What we forget is that what we're learning may not be what the other person is learning. It's all about love, but the way we go about learning it, the way the lessons are delivered, are unique to our own paths. But each person on each side of the equation is learning something. There's a great mutuality, if we recognize the wisdom in our struggles. As soon as we think it's all about the other (it's their fault, I had nothing to do with this), we deny what we are supposed to learn, what our lesson is in the relationship . . . always about love.

When we come from that wellspring of love, we are centered and grounded in that love. That is why love is so powerful. We can't be knocked off our center when we are anchored in that willingness to do what is most loving, for ourselves and then for others. Then we are anchored to our Higher Self, the Love we are. We can be compassionate when someone doesn't understand. They don't need to understand our path, our life. It's for us to understand, not them. Those who truly love us respect that we are willing to take loving care of ourselves, even if they don't always get what they want. Someone who wants us to do what is damaging or detrimental to us is not loving us mutually. Someone who guilts us about how we need to take care of ourselves is not loving us, they are wanting to bully and control. And they may not realize what they are doing, or may not be willing to hear how their behavior feels. And we may wish they would be different or understand. It can be very sad when people are not willing to be in their highest integrity, their Highest Self, the Love that we all are. Because ultimately, when we are not loving, the first person we hurt is our own self.

Sometimes we don't know what is the most loving thing to do. Then we ask for help, from our Higher Self (our innate wisdom and Love) and all of the Universe, which is at our beck and call as we are always indivisibly connected. We have to be willing to hear the answer, no matter what it is. We may not ask until we're ready to hear the answer. Eventually, in every situation, no matter how long it takes, we finally hear that which is the most loving thing we can do for ourselves, right now. And we will act on it at just the right time, in just the right way, so that what we do is for our highest good and that of all concerned.

All day long, for everything that comes up, I ask the question: What is the most loving thing for me to do right now? This daily practice opens the channel to my Higher Self, my inner wisdom. I hear my answers more clearly, more effortlessly. I am sometimes surprised that I have the answer right there. I just had to ask.

When we don't know what to do, we first apply Love in some way, shape or form. This might mean we just say I need help being kind, compassionate, loving to myself or another. Help me to come from a loving place for myself and others. I'm willing (at least 51 percent) to do the most loving thing right now. Start there, with willingness. It's OK to be unknowing. Even if we don't feel it, remembering that we are Love is our guiding light, our lantern in the dark. Its beacon will illuminate our hearts and shine a light wherever we need it.

Everything, truly, is all about Love. And Love is Light.

What's True?

We like to tell ourselves stories. We think we know what other people are thinking. We make things up and then believe what we are telling ourselves. All of this behavior causes us to suffer. We step off our paths when we think about what others are doing and thinking. And, after all, what other people think of us is none of our business. All we can control are our thoughts, our paths. This is the Law of Individuality.

Just like we can check in often and ask ourselves: What's the most loving thing for me to do in this situation? What's really true here? What's really happening?

We know when we get off track, deviate from our paths or are not true to ourselves because we feel the discomfort or uneasiness. We feel icky (yes, that's the clinical term, lol). The body is a great vehicle of communication, because when we transgress ourselves or someone has transgressed us, we feel it somewhere in our bodies. A therapist told me many years ago that if you feel like you've been punched in the stomach, you have. We can trust that there is something underneath the feeling in the body. Trust that inner voice, the Higher Self, that speaks to us through the body.

IT'S ALL ABOUT LOVE

People are not always kind or loving. When we are hurt or blaming, we can ask ourselves: What's true here? And then be willing to hear the answer, no matter what it is. And then do what is most loving, first for ourselves—for our highest good, and the highest good of all concerned. It is our responsibility to be kind and loving to ourselves, first. In that loving space, we can hear what's really true, not the story we may want to tell ourselves. And then we can respond in the most loving way that supports us, even if someone else isn't supporting us. Hearing the truth about ourselves—and others—helps us to be more compassionate and loving to us . . . which fills us up and allows us to spill love over to others. And then we're all uplifted into more light and love.

TLC for Your Beloved Self

It was a stormy day when I first read the poem "Clearing" by Martha Postlewaite.

Listen to this beautiful phrase: " . . . in the dense forest of your life . . . wait there patiently, until the song that is your life falls into your own cupped hands and you recognize and greet it."

Stormy weather often provides time for reflection and self-care as we hunker down and stay close to home. We take loving care of ourselves before giving ourselves to the world. One of the meditations in the Reiki classes that I teach includes the phrase: "We fill up, and **then** pour our resources to the world."

Storms can give us some down time to be gentle with ourselves and practice some loving kindness to our beloved selves. Maybe we can make some space in the density of life and the song of our life will fall into our cupped hands. As you would hold, comfort and cradle a child, a beloved pet or a dear friend in times of stress, hold yourself tenderly, be there for yourself, listen to the song in your heart. You are your own beloved.

Clearing

Do not try to save

the whole world

or do anything grandiose.

Instead, create a clearing

in the dense forest of your life

and wait there

patiently,

until the song

that is your life

falls into your own cupped hands

and you recognize and greet it.

Only then will you know

how to give yourself

to this world

so worthy of rescue.

Autumn Reflections

Autumn is a time to gather, to harvest what we have grown, understood and resolved during the summer. As the energy begins to contract in the yin of autumn, we keep what will sustain us in the coming quieter, darker time of hibernation and re-nourishment, and let go what no longer serves us.

In Chinese Medicine, fall is the time of the metal element, and the lung and large intestine channels of energy. We use metal to create infrastructure. And sometimes the old infrastructure has to be torn down to make way for the new. In the fall, we "gather in" what we have grown during the spring and summer and sort through all of that to keep what will serve and nourish us in the winter to come. We let go that which is not up to snuff, that which will not nourish us during hibernation and rest. There is often grief in letting go, but letting go is necessary to make room for more good. We must create the space to allow for the receiving.

Michael Gach is a wonderful acupressure teacher and says this about the metal element, the energy of lung and large intestine meridians (the channels of energy) and autumn:

Imagine your body's vast network,

Take energy into your lungs,

Let go of all that is unnecessary.

Receive and store energy, eliminate wastes.

The skin breathes . . .

Spicy foods open the pores:

Ginger, onions and garlic.

Let go of what is inside,

Clearing mucus and toxins

Like the falling leaves, let go;

Grieving releases a loss.

Deepen your breathing,

Channel your energy;

Consciously use the tools you have been given.

Autumn is thought of as the time of letting come and letting go, which are the functions of our lungs and large intestines. We take a breath, and then go of our breath to allow us to take the next breath. We eat, and then let go of what we have eaten and digested to make room for our next meal. Energetically, we make room to let come what we need to sustain us through the next season of yin, before the yang of spring. The time of the metal element is a time of restructuring, tearing down what doesn't support us, so our new, stronger infrastructure can begin to be planned and eventually built.

Sometimes it is time to let go of people in our lives. Hindu guru Neem Karoli Baba said: "Don't throw anyone out of your heart." Sometimes the only way we can remain loving is to let go of contact with particular beings. Sometimes the best and wisest thing to do is to send loving-kindness from afar. This letting go may be accompanied by grief, and it may be for our highest good, and that of all concerned.

I love fall and winter. I love the internal times. Today is a perfect time to simply affirm: I let go of whatever I need to release. I make room to receive whatever is for my highest good.

We let go, we let come. We don't have to worry about the how, or the details. We will be guided as to what our part is. We stay willing. We trust. We rest. Happy autumn!

Loving Yourself

I love and accept myself exactly as I am.

— Louise Hay

We are always in the process of learning to love ourselves, just as we are, right now, in the present moment. It's not a matter of, I'll love myself when such and such happens. That is how we suffer. Louise Hay spent her life teaching about loving ourselves. She was a Master Metaphysician, a Master of Love, and a mentor for me. Her teachings about love live on through her books and writings.

One of the first books I suggest to people is Louise's *You Can Heal Your Life*. It's a metaphysical primer that is a great starting place. I go back to it continually. Here are some wise words from a wise and loving being: "If you do not love yourself totally, wholly, and fully, somewhere along the way you learned not to. You can unlearn it. Start being kind to yourself now."

While we may not feel loving as we recite the meditation below, if we willingly keep at it, day by day, we are moved to a feeling of love. We lay in the gossamer wings of good feeling each time we say it. Eventually, without even knowing it, we reach 51 percent of loving good feeling for our own being, our heart opens to our self and we fall in love with who we are, just as we are in this very moment.

Many years ago, I began a simple mantra to help me love myself. I would say, just twice a day: I love and accept who I am and who I've created myself to be over all the years of my life. At first, it didn't feel true at all. That didn't matter. I just persisted, gently, and after about six weeks (after a lifetime of not loving myself) I said it one more time. And this time, my heart opened. I saw my true self in my eyes—the self of Love that we all are—and I fell in love. With me. And my life changed in that moment, because I was finally willing to see myself through the eyes of love. And I didn't even know I had reached the 51 percent.

Here is Louise Hay's Meditation. Find the words that work for you. And just be willing.

I Accept All That I've Created for Myself

I love and accept myself exactly as I am. I support myself, trust myself, and accept myself wherever I am. I can be within the love of my own heart. I place my hand over my heart and feel the love that is there. I know there is plenty of room for me to accept myself right here and now. I accept my body, my weight, my height, my appearance, my sexuality, and my experiences. I accept all that I have created for myself—my past and my present. I am willing to allow my future to happen. I am a Divine, Magnificent Expression of Life, and I deserve the very best. I accept this for myself now. I accept miracles. I accept healing. I accept wholeness. And most of all, I accept myself. I am precious, and I cherish who I am. And so it is.

Keep it Simple

I often think about simplicity. We spend so much time sorting through issues in our lives, which is necessary when that's what we need to do. Sometimes, deeply buried splinters rise up to the surface and demand attention. And periodically, we come to a clear place, like a still pool. And we glimpse how simple it all is. Not that it's easy to get there. But ultimately, it's simple.

So, I want to keep this simple. We can distill our inner work down to letting go, and making space to receive more good than we can imagine. Letting go, and allowing, even welcoming, whatever is for our highest good . . . not knowing what that is. Letting go, and feeling that exquisite present-ness which brings peace to the moment. It's a choice.

So, whenever you are feeling discordant, not harmonious or not peaceful, pause. Take a breath. Breath connects us with Spirit (inhalation=inspiration=In Spirit). Review what you are holding on to, or turning over in your mind. If it isn't useful or loving, if you aren't minding your own business or you are off your path and on someone else's path, if you are thinking of someone else and what they are doing or thinking, let go. Just be willing. Just forgive yourself. Be kind to yourself. Have compassion for yourself. Hold the intention to let go and say, I let go. I let go of whatever I'm holding on to that is not serving my highest good. You don't even need to know what it is.

Eventually you will let go, when your willingness and feeling of letting go reaches 51 percent. You may not know when that happens, but just by making that choice over and over and by being willing and compassionate for how we hold on to a myriad of stuff as humans, you will make it happen. Every time we are willing to let go, a bit of what we have been carrying around with us is emptied out of our energy field. At some point, we just have a wholesale release. We reach 51 percent or more. And we move into the present and into peace.

Just try it. Make some room in your life for the Universe to give you the blessings you want, the blessings that are for your highest good. Make some room at your inn.

It's Simple . . . Not Easy

Through all my writings about simplicity, and trying to break this metaphysical stuff down to its bare bones so it is usable and applicable in daily life, I always realize the mechanics are simple. . .and putting them into practice is not easy.

I've been studying and using metaphysics—the loving energy we are beyond our physical bodies—for some 45-plus years. It's been a long, slow, evolutionary process of trial and error, practice and realization. At the end of the day, it all becomes very simple. But it took all the years, all the steps, all the missteps that turned out to be perfectly necessary to arrive at the understanding of how simple it really is.

Life is always happening. Details and people change, but life is always happening. We can't stop the waves of life; we learn to surf better. What that means is we finally decide that the only thing we can control is our response to all that happens. Some of what happens in life will feel bad, some will feel good. But ultimately, after all the practice of living years of life, something gives. We decide it's too hard to react to everything, to judge everything. And we have our history that everything works out—one way or the other. And we somehow get through everything. Everything is energy, and energy is always moving forward, and actually moving forward to the good. Although it is hard to see that, at times . . . so we just learn to trust it before we see it. Sometimes the good is that we learn from what happened. Sometimes the good is that we develop compassion for ourselves and others. And no matter how bad something feels, eventually we feel better, because everything does changes.

So that's how we keep things simple. Life happens, we notice. Just like in meditation when we notice we have a thought of some kind, and we say, *thinking, thought, fear, anxiety*. We notice, we let it go. In life, something happens that is upsetting, and we might react. We forgive ourselves, if our reaction makes us suffer. We take a breath. We remember everything is energy and energy is not static. Energy always moves. Eventually, whatever dire situation we are dealing with will change, will morph. This, too, shall pass. We make a choice to let go of whatever we are thinking that is not helping us to respond to the situation, and choose our response, knowing we are not in this life alone. Our response is our response-ability—our responsibility. We are held in the palm of the Universe, fully supported, loved, part of All That Is. We can ask, cry out for help and be willing to receive it. Maybe it won't look like what we imagined, but it will be for our highest good.

And then the hardest part happens. We sit in trust. We trust it out. We don't know when the right time is for something to change. The hardest part is to feel peace in each moment, to be willing to feel some joy or ease even in the midst of the stresses of life. It might be as simple as to have compassion for what we are going through, or taking in the blue sky, or the soft rain, a loving text, a hug from a friend, or hugging the cat. There is something we can do to lift our energy, to connect to the love that we are. That loving energy is buoyant and if we make the smallest effort, have the tiniest willingness to allow it in, it fills us up and floats us forward just where we need to go.

And we start with the simplest thing in the world. We take a breath.

Abundance Revisited

It's always good to have an abundance of down time. Lots of things come up for which I normally wouldn't have the energetic or mental space. So even before Hurricanes Florence and then Michael gave me a good excuse to hunker down and laze around physically, I was tossing the idea of abundance around in my mentality once again, checking within to see how I really felt about being an indivisible part of the inherent, natural abundance of the Universe.

Abundance is a state of mind and the truth of our being, AND we need to do our part to allow that sense of abundance so the pictures of abundance flow into our lives.

We may be exhausted, burned out, and in between jobs, or have unexpected time off. We feel guilty if we take time off to rebuild and rest. We feel guilty if we don't rush into working at something, anything. If we are having the thought or feeling that we are running out of money and have to work immediately to get more money, even at something that we know is not right for us, THAT feeling of lack, restriction and anxiety will close off our flow of abundance. The abundance is already there, because Spirit is infinitely abundant and we see the evidence of that in Nature all around us. We are an indivisible part of Spirit, so we are also an indivisible part of the abundance. And Spirit is infinitely abundant!

Money doesn't flow from a job or a boss, really. It flows from the infinite abundance of Spirit through the channel of a business or a boss or work . . . or the lottery! Whatever is for your highest good. We have to have a visible channel for money to appear because we are in a visible world. Although money can also just appear on the sidewalk! But probably not the amount of money you are thinking of.

It's all about Love, like everything is. How does Love relate to money? Love is the energy of the Universe. Money is one of the visible symbols in this earth plane of the circulation of good feeling, the currency, the movement (like a current) of love and good feeling— always to yourself first. Part of loving ourselves is being willing to do whatever is necessary . . . with a willing heart. We may need to do something that is not our be all and end all work, but all work is meaningful somehow and if we have a grateful heart for the work, it may be the energetic stepping stone to the work that does make our heart sing.

What is important in dealing with money is what you are feeling 51 percent of the time. Are you holding back your good feeling 51 percent of the time? You may be fearful and worried 49 percent of the time, and still trusting and taking loving care of yourself 51 percent of the time. If you are not seeing abundance/money in your life, you are not at the 51 percent and you have to ask yourself, where might I be holding back my good feeling? We know. We might ask, is the way I am spending money truly loving to me? If I spend all of my money, how is that loving? If I cannot pay my bills, my rent, my mortgage, is that loving?

There is a discernment between thoughtless extravagance and trusting the flow of abundance of the Universe. If we think that we don't have to be responsible about money, that we can spend all we want, that we don't have to take responsibility for ourselves because the Universe will take care of us, then we are not doing our part, and not taking loving care of ourselves.

We are human, so the fear of lack of enough money can sometimes be overwhelming. Whenever we are faced with fear, worry or anxiety, we apply love. We take loving care of ourselves, do our part to bring in money, saving what we can, if we can, enjoying life in a reasonable fashion, spending money with an attitude of joy when it feels good, and not doing spending when it doesn't feel good or we feel guilty spending.

So, this is the crux: if how we are spending money and thinking and feeling about money is really loving, really for our highest good and the highest good of all concerned, it will feel good. We will welcome more money, a symbol of love and good feeling! If we say, I am just going to spend what I want and not be thoughtful about it, and we have an underlying fear (of more than 51 percent) then all we're doing is spending money AND closing down the flow of good feeling and closing down the flow of more money. It's the 51 percent feeling of ease and trust and confidence that I am taking care of myself in the most loving way, doing everything necessary to take loving care of myself, that greases the gears of the Universe and allows the flow to continue. It's all up to us and whether we are circulating good feeling, love and trust, taking loving care of ourselves in every way necessary, 51 percent of the time. So, it's the doing our part and coming to the good feeling that brings forth the picture of the abundance that is already there in Spirit, of which we are already a part.

We practice taking a break from financial worry. All worry does is close down the flow. You can approach financial issues with care and reason and observe how much worry you have, and just keep it under 51 percent. We are human, we are going to worry. But don't take a siesta from doing what's loving for you. That is essential to do every day. And spending everything AND having more than 51 percent fear will grind the gears to a halt and stop the flow.

Whenever we have a lack of money, we need to ask ourselves where we are stopping our flow of good feeling. Sometimes money seems to land in our lap so easily from unexpected places. This is a reflection of the abundant good feeling we engender in some way, through our spiritual work, our belief that we are taken care of, asking for help (out loud or silently) and being willing to receive, or just a sense that it is easy to make money! Yes, some people do feel that way. The money is always the picture of the abundance of good feeling we are circulating. The more we take loving care of ourselves, the more good feeling we have to circulate.

We need to be in the feeling (51 percent) that the abundance is already here, has already happened. It truly has already happened in

Spirit, it's ALWAYS there, more than enough, infinitely! To allow the appearance of that in our lives, we have to feel 51 percent that it's already manifested, appeared, projected, into our life. Not, I will win the lottery, but I already have more than plenty! And we don't have to figure out the how. That is the job of Spirit/Source/the All/Universe/God. Our job is to do what is loving (our responsibility in the process, we don't abdicate our responsibility for our lives), do whatever is necessary, and get to the 51 percent feeling of, it's already done, easily, perfectly. That allows the solution, the resolution, the manifestation, to drop in our laps. We have to do our job in our thoughts and in the world, and let go to make space to receive the answer. That's how it works. So, we are on the right track when we do our part, trust, and let go. But if we let go and still are overwhelmed by fear, we still close the flow. Affirmations and mantras don't do anything in and of themselves. They are meant to be used to move us toward the FEELING—51 percent—that what we are affirming has already happened. We feel it, trust it, before we see it.

So how do we have good feeling when we don't have enough money? We can't think and feel: I would like more money, and when I have it, I will feel better. We must feel good NOW. Our primary life work—our true mission—is circulating, promoting, flowing, allowing good feeling and love, to ourselves first. When we do that, we fill up and spill over that good feeling to everyone else. We must find peace where we are. When I am willing to feel that I love my life, I love me, I love where I am in my life, I am grateful for everything . . . then I feel filled, abundant, more than enough. That is first, and then the money flows from there.

We find something that is abundant in our lives. I always think of my abundant irises and the abundant love in my life and I know I am already wealthy in Spirit. And then I see the projection of having what I need and desire in my visible life.

Life is a balancing act as we monitor and feel our levels of fear/worry/anxiety and love/trust/flow. Love is the least amount of fear. Fear is the least amount of love. We just keep applying love/trust/flow to deal with the fear/worry/anxiety. And we become very skilled at asking: Is this the most loving thing I can do for myself? You will know the answer in your heart of hearts.

A Refrigerator Can Be More Than Just a Refrigerator

Everything in the visible world is a symbol of the energy moving in the invisible. Not that we always understand it, or need to understand it. Sometimes the symbol just means that life is energy and energy always moves and changes, and we just need to accept that impermanence. Sometimes, I find it useful to look at seemingly mundane occurrences and see if it relates to how I am moving energy on my own path, in my own mind and my own life.

Louise Hay includes a guide to metaphysical diagnosis at the back of all her books. Over her years of working with people, she came up with a list of physical ailments that she related to possibilities of how people might be congesting their energy movement, along with suggestions of ways to think that might flow the energy better in that particular situation. Whenever I have something physical going on, I always look at her list. It is up to us to decide if something resonates or fits; we have responsibility for our own life and discernment is important. We are not meant to blindly follow anyone else's way of thinking. We need to decide what is true for us. We are told we each need to work out our own salvation, use our reason and come to conclusions for ourselves.

That being said, there have been times I read what she has to say about knee issues, for example, and I would think, I can't see where I am in the grip of ego, fear or stubbornness. Silly me. Her new thought pattern is: *"I am flexible and flowing. Forgiveness. Understanding. Compassion. I bend and flow with ease, and all is well."* So maybe, just maybe, it did fit!

Again, no matter what Louise Hay said out of her vast experience, it was still my work to apply this to me—if the shoe fits, so to speak. But always, the solution is to apply love: *"I am flexible and flowing. Forgiveness. Understanding. Compassion. I bend and flow with ease, and all is well."* Apply love to myself, apply compassion for whatever inflexibility, fear, stubbornness I held on to long enough to create a pattern in my physical body.

This is not to blame or punish ourselves for what we experience physically. This is to show us how powerful we are as energetic beings and in using energy, if not to create something, to respond to something lovingly. Not that the loving response will take away the manifestation of illness, but it will help us respond lovingly to whatever we are experiencing without judgment or harshness, but with sweetness, compassion, understanding and love. This helps us treat ourselves like we would a dear friend, a child, or a beloved four-legged fur baby.

A simple way of looking at this mind-body connection (with compassion) is when my neck is stiff, how am I being stiff-necked? How am I being rigid and unbending and in that resistance or resentment, causing myself pain which shows up in my body? Again, not in a punishing, berating manner, but lovingly, kindly, with curiosity. And you may not have an answer, and that's OK. What's important is to be loving and kind to ourselves and do whatever is appropriate to get relief. And along the way, sometimes many years later, we may have an inkling or an intuition about what mental pattern we may have been perpetuating that could have contributed to our issue. Again, what's important is being loving and kind to ourselves, not giving ourselves the third degree. It's the love that heals, not the answer.

And back to the refrigerator. Some years ago, when our refrigerator stopped working, we were told it might have been due to a power surge. The solution was to get a new refrigerator—and a surge suppressor. And after taking care of that, I reflected on how the energy spike that did in our fridge might relate to me. I knew I had been feeling up and down, very tired, working too hard. I felt like I was breaking down in some way and, in hindsight, clearly not taking loving care of myself, although I wasn't really aware of it at the time.

We got a new refrigerator on Dec. 30, 2012. In January 2013, a lump appeared on my left arm. By February, I had been diagnosed with a malignant tumor that turned out to be sarcoma. Two surgeries, radiation and five years of recovery followed, which entailed learning about how to take more loving care of myself than I could imagine.

I did ask my Higher Self, my inner wisdom, what the cancer may have represented. Not that I brought this on as punishment for something, but I was willing to explore the possibility that this physical manifestation might have wisdom, guidance or teaching for me. Since everything is about Love, the main question was, would this help me see where I might have been unloving to myself in the past, and help guide me to be more loving to myself in the future. It was one of those "wake up" moments.

And I say recovery took five years because not only did the effects of surgery and radiation and overwork ease over those five years, slowly, bit by bit, but it also took five years for me to work with each Pillar of Health (Right rest, Right nutrition, Right movement, Right relationship within and without) and come to a better understanding about what it truly means to take loving care of myself and continually apply it, as best I can. And being human, sometimes I do a better job than at other times.

Since Love is infinite, limitless and eternal, our work of learning to love ourselves is continuous throughout our lifetime. We're never "done." It actually is wonderful that every day is a continuing opportunity to love ourselves more than we can imagine. And we may even learn to enjoy the adventure.

The Heart of the Universe
or . . . We are Love

We are Love. The heart of the Universe opens and expresses everything, including us. Love begets Love. We are Love.

Once we are expressed, what are we to do with our lives? We love. Our true work, our true mission in life is to circulate love and good feeling to ourselves first. We fill up with that love and it spills over to everyone and everything around us. Why?

Because it feels good to us. Because if we don't circulate that love, the heart of the Universe breaks a little. We are created out of love (by the Universe if not by the people giving birth to us) and the Universe/Spirit/Love asks us to acknowledge that. To feel the love we are inherently. To know we are Love just the way we are. No matter what we accomplish or don't accomplish, we are still Love. And we are still meant to love, which means sending love out to the Universe. It's as easy as sending out our breath. Just exhale the love we are to the All. Even if we can't feel it, we can know it. And then we are meant to receive that love as it circles back.

The Universe depends on us to send that love out for its expansion. And in that expanded state, it gives even more love back to us, with our next inhale. If we don't realize we are inherently love, and don't circulate that love intentionally, to ourselves and others as best we can in the moment, we starve the Universe a little bit. The Universe says: Oh, I could have expanded a bit more with your love, so I'd have even more to send to you and everyone. But as you deny the love you are, you deny the All and everyone and everything in it of the benefit of even more love. All you have to do is own the love you are and send it out. Just with a breath. Just as we can starve our human bodies of the nutrition we need by not paying attention to what lovingly feeds and nourishes us, we can starve the Universe of our contribution of love. The more we realize the Love we are and breathe that into the Universe, the more love there is for us and everyone to receive with our very next breath.

This is why we must receive, both in our human lives and in Spirit. We are not meant to only give. We are meant to receive or we don't complete the circle of love.

This is what we have a lifetime for, to learn all of this. To practice all of this. To suffuse everything we do with this practice. And that's how we feel joy.

The heart of the Universe is infinitely expanding into limitless love. We already are that love. We love. And we are loved.

We Are Not Alone

I have an ongoing daily dialogue with my guides. I also call them my angels or my protectors in spirit. My Higher Self is part of this entourage or group that I talk to, consult and call on regularly. What does this mean? And how do you do it or why would you want to do it?

I like things to be simple, effective, direct. We want to call on our guides for . . . well, everything! Our guides, our higher selves, are part of each of us: the higher, wiser part of us. If there is a willing being always at hand ready to help with absolutely anything and everything, no matter how trivial or mundane we may judge it—and the biggest things, too—why wouldn't we call on that being and make life easier? As the saying goes, two heads are better than one. How about an infinite Universe at our beck and call?

It's easy to feel alone in this human world. But we are part of Spirit, Divine, even as we are manifested in this human body. That's why we are always inherently Love, because Spirit is inherently Love, and we are an indivisible part of that. So, we are never alone! We just can't always see or hear or feel the "rest" of the Universe of which we are a part. That doesn't make it any less real or available to us. And make no mistake, the

Universe is available to help us with absolutely anything and everything! We just have to ask and receive. And trusting that we are entitled to ask and trusting we will be answered makes the process even smoother.

We all have ways that we think of God, Source, the Universe, All That Is, Oneness. It doesn't really matter how we think of it or what we call it as long as we remember that we are part and parcel of the Oneness, indivisible with all Love and Beingness. We have all the qualities of whatever we think of as God. We just are not all of it. It takes everything to make up the Oneness. The quality of the Oneness is Love.

And when someone loves us unconditionally, they are there for us. And the Universe is always there for us. It's like we're joined at the hip and when we ask for something, there always has to be a response, although it may not look like what we are expecting. When we push, the Universe is pushed. When we pull, the Universe is pulled. We can't be disconnected. We can feel like we are disconnected, but we never are in reality.

And it doesn't matter if we hear anything or are aware of anything. Our words and thoughts do not fall into a void or a vacuum. We are heard and responded to. So, it's so important to always ask for what we need and know there will be a response even though we can't necessarily count on what it will look like. The response will always be for our highest good.

Years ago, I had a vision of many people pushing against a fence. I came to realize they were guides, or how I think of the helping aspect of the Universe. They told me: *We are here for you! We are here to help you! But you have free will; you have to ask! Now go and tell people to ask and trust they will be heard and will receive what they need.*

So that's what I've been doing for a very long time. I tell people to ask for help with everything. And expect to receive a response! And I remind myself of this, too. I make it a practice to send a request out for everything that requires some consideration. Why not use all of my Being and All of the All since it's available to me? A wiser mind than just my own human mind will weigh in, if invited. And I mean, I ask about everything. Should I do this now? What should I eat? What would feel loving now? How should I adjust my schedule? Should I make or cancel this appointment? What about another glass of wine? How about this bill? It's not that I can't think for myself or make my own decisions. It's about giving up being on auto-pilot and really asking: What is the most loving thing I can do here? What is the most loving action, the most loving decision, for my highest good and that of all concerned?

If I just use my human mind, I may not come up with the most loving course of action. Sometimes, the most loving course of action is no action! But human mind often wants to do *something*. Our Divine mind will be more thoughtful, more aware, more conscious more loving, more true about what's loving. We just have to take a moment, take a breath, and ask.

How do we hear our angels/guides/protectors in spirit/the Universe? We all have had that feeling of, don't do that, do this only to ignore our inner voice and regret the outcome. We knew, we felt, we didn't pay attention. The answer can come in an instant as if it were just dropped in our awareness; or we read something, or see something, or someone says something, or all of a sudden, we just realize the answer. The more we practice this, the easier, the smoother the process becomes. The inner voice can be a still, small voice. We need practice to hear it and practice to trust it.

And sometimes, I actually do hear a voice. But mostly, it's a sense, or an impression, or suddenly the answer is just there. All of a sudden, I will feel, *time to do this now!* And I always ask for crystal clear answers. Because even after all this time, I can be rather hard-headed. And then I ask for help to be compassionate to myself.

Sometimes the answer is, just bring a loving response to this situation, difficult as it is, and it will all unfold in just the right way in just the right time. Trust. Because after all, it is All About Love.

What Is Love?

A friend once asked me; "So what is love, really? How would you define it?" She felt that appreciation embraced the concept of love, which is very true.

When I think of love, I always think of loving ourselves first. If we don't feel that, it's hard to feel it for anyone else. And that takes a long time to learn. We are given innumerable opportunities every day to practice, to choose, to be kind and loving to ourselves. And the more we practice that, the easier it is to extend that to others.

One of the ways we don't love ourselves is by doing things or acting in ways that do not serve us. We may take a rigid stance in a discussion with a loved one. Being rigid and unbending, being unwilling to see how our behavior hurts or affects another, even if we don't understand it, ultimately denies us closeness and intimacy. That is being unloving.

We all have our own ways of not being loving to ourselves. They might include working too hard, ignoring the Four Pillars of Health (Right rest, Right nutrition, Right movement, Right relationship within and without), holding anger, or not staying on our path (not minding our own business). We may ignore the messages our body and Higher

Self are giving us, not make space and time to be present with ourselves, hold ourselves to impossible standards of perfection and, thus, do the same to others, and tell ourselves stories about a person or a situation. These are some common ways we all can be unloving to ourselves. Any of them sound familiar to you? I certainly can relate to them.

At one point while I was working to release some of my own unloving ways of being and thinking, I reached out to my guides for help, which I do for practically everything. They answered me immediately, clearly and unequivocally. Bring grace to bear, they said. No matter what the issue or situation, bring grace to bear. Another way of saying this is bring love to bear. Bring kindness to bear. Bring your highest self, highest integrity, to every situation. Bring ease, bring compassion, willingness. These are all facets of grace and love.

One way we love is by expressing our skills, talents, faculties and abilities, expressing who we are and what is within us in our own inimitable way. We are expressed, birthed by the Universe, and we also want to express in some way, birth something or someone. It is said in metaphysics that the quality of the Universe, of life, is love. And love wants to, needs to, be expressed. The quantity is perfection. Not being perfect, but the perfection of everyone and everything expressing itself in its own unique way.

When it comes to relationships, sometimes love is being willing to love someone in the way that feels loving to them, if it doesn't compromise us. We can compromise, we just can't compromise our integrity, ourselves. When someone we love tells us what would feel loving to them, we can decide if we can do that, if it would be for our highest good. If we are being loving to us, it will be loving to the other person. If we do something out of obligation with resentment, it will not feel loving to us or the person with whom we are in relationship. This is being willing to do what serves us, as we love another. When we are not willing to do what serves us, what is for our highest good, that is also known as getting in our own way. When we are unbending and unyielding, we are not flexible enough to put our arms around ourselves, much less another. We often get to experience and practice this in relationships. Relationships are the vehicles to really learn about love, whether it be friendships or more intimate relationships. Or we may think we have it all figured out and it's hard for us to admit we still have issues to work on—another way of being rigid and unyielding.

Ram Dass says it well: "If you think you're enlightened, go spend a week with your family."

Love is also willingness. Love and willingness are the keys to healing. And the willingness is always—remember how we started—willingness to do what is most loving for ourselves, so we can then fill up and spill over that love. As Richard Rohr says: " . . . grace cannot enter without an opening from our side."

Sometimes the willingness guides us to let go. We can love by letting go of expectation of ourselves or another. We can be willing to see how people actually are and not what we would wish them to be or the story we are telling ourselves about them. In that clarity, we can decide what is most loving for us. Remember the old saying, friendships (or relationships) are for a reason, a season or forever? Sometimes the most loving thing to do is to leave a relationship. If we can't be loving, we won't circulate love or good feeling, to ourselves or other. And that is our primary mission in this lifetime.

It's not enough just to say we love ourselves or someone else. This is why the expression, the quantity, of love is so important. That expression will be individual, but there must be an expression of our love. The Universe didn't stay unexpressed as an idea; it burst forth expressed in infinite ways. As part of the Universe, we too must express the Love we are, in our own ways to be sure, but express we must.

Make no mistake: loving oneself is not the same as being selfish or self-absorbed. If something is only good for us and not good for others, then it is not loving. If we cannot look beyond ourselves and be mutually loving with the appropriate people in our lives who are truly loving, then we must ask ourselves: How much do I really love and care for myself? How good do I really feel about myself if I can't return pure love when it is offered from the right person?

If we put all of our love to others and deny ourselves that same care and love, it is not a measure of how loving we are but how much we need to love ourselves, because ultimately, we will empty our vessel giving all of our love away and not giving any to ourselves. We need to receive the love as well as give it. If we continually give but don't think we are worthy of receiving that same love, we wind up emptying the vessel and scraping the bottom of the barrel and then feeling resentful about those that we are supposedly loving. We think we aren't getting enough back but truly we didn't give enough to ourselves in the first place. We need to give from a full reservoir; we can't give from an empty place. When we are truly filling ourselves first, receiving the love that's always available from the All first, and then love others, it enables us to recognize whether we are in a mutually loving relationship—or not. Then we can make a decision about what's the most loving thing for us to do. It truly is All About Love.

And then we have to remember that everyone is truly doing the best they can. What does that mean? Even if someone is unwilling or unable or seemingly incapable of loving themselves, which then expresses in being unkind to another, that is what is possible for them at that moment. Even if they are making a choice to be unloving or mean or cruel, even in that choice, they may know better, intellectually—or not—and still justify their unloving actions, indignantly and righteously. Until we find and feel the love within ourselves, we can't express it. Not that we sanction, condone or accept this behavior. We don't love bad behavior. But we need to remember that every human has a Divine part, our Higher Self. And, we have free will. So, while our Higher Self is pure love, and that is what we love in everyone, our human self is very capable of exercising free will to be cruel and unloving in a myriad of ways. And we don't love that hurtfulness. We may understand they are choosing not to change anything, or may not know they can change or know how. Our responsibility is to love ourselves, and we may need to remove ourselves from their presence, in love for ourselves. No one else knows what is loving for us the way we do.

If all this sounds like a lot of work, well, loving and loving well is an effort. It's part of the grand adventure that life is. We are human, as well as Divine, so we're not going to love perfectly. Remember the quality and quantity? We already are inherently, intrinsically Love. We already are the quality of the Universe since we spring out of the energy of the Universe. It is up to us to express the quantity of Love, which is our individual expression through all of our facets of the jewel that we are. And different facets are "lit up" and expressed at different times of our lives. That expression is what brings us joy. And feeling joy is the purpose of life. That is why we love. There's no better work.

This is what a lifetime is for, to be aware of and work through all of these issues: what we are (Love); why we are here (to circulate that love and good feeling, to ourselves first, through the expression of our skills, faculties, talents and abilities); and all for the purpose of being in joy.

James Finley, a contemplative teacher and writer and a retired clinical psychologist, often says: "You are not what has happened to you. Only Love has the final word in who you are."

And then when we're done with what we're going to do in this lifetime, well, we're done! But until then . . . we're still doing the work, every day. Right up until our very last day on this earth.

World Peace

Let's start a movement. PEACE WITHIN, PEACE WITHOUT. The world out there reflects the world inside of us. If each of us takes just a moment here and there during the day to say to ourselves, peace within, peace without, we will send increasing waves of loving energy from our microcosm into the macrocosm, from us to the Universe, sweeping across everyone on the planet in the process—and beyond.

Can you imagine what would happen if 51 percent of the world simply uttered, peace within, peace without at the same moment?! Without knowing the how or the details, the world would change in that instant through the healing power of loving energy that we choose to embrace and mobilize. When we stop warring within, we stop warring out there in the world. We think "that war" isn't our war, but it's everyone's war. We are an indivisible part of everyone and everything.

Align with your loving being, your true self, just through willingness and intent, and radiate that most powerful loving force to yourself, through yourself and the world. As you do, ask everyone in the world to open their hearts to Love. That's it. Please join me. PEACE WITHIN, PEACE WITHOUT. Thank you!

Printed in the United States
By Bookmasters